Teaching Strategies
for All Teachers

Teaching Strategies for All Teachers

Enhancing the Most Significant Variable

Andrew P. Johnson

ROWMAN & LITTLEFIELD
Lanham • Boulder • New York • London

Published by Rowman & Littlefield
A wholly owned subsidiary of The Rowman & Littlefield Publishing Group, Inc.
4501 Forbes Boulevard, Suite 200, Lanham, Maryland 20706
www.rowman.com

Unit A, Whitacre Mews, 26–34 Stannary Street, London SE11 4AB

British Library Cataloguing in Publication Information Available

Library of Congress Cataloging-in-Publication Data
Names: Johnson, Andrew P. (Andrew Paul), author.
Title: Teaching strategies for all teachers : enhancing the most significant variable /
    Andrew P. Johnson.
Description: Lanham, Maryland : Rowman & Littlefield, [2017] | Includes
    bibliographical references.
Identifiers: LCCN 2017029117 (print) | LCCN 2017040634 (ebook) |
    ISBN 9781475834680 (Electronic) | ISBN 9781475834666 (cloth : alk. paper) |
    ISBN 9781475834673 (pbk. : alk. paper)
Subjects: LCSH: Effective teaching. | Teaching—Methodology.
Classification: LCC LB1025.3 (ebook) | LCC LB1025.3 .J57 2017 (print) |
    DDC 371.102—dc23
LC record available at https://lccn.loc.gov/2017029117

♾™ The paper used in this publication meets the minimum requirements of American
National Standard for Information Sciences—Permanence of Paper for Printed Library
Materials, ANSI/NISO Z39.48–1992.

Printed in the United States of America

This book is dedicated to the memory of Mr. Clayton Jorgenson. He was a teacher, principal, Boy Scout troop leader, and a very good man

Contents

Preface

My purpose for writing this book initially was to provide a vehicle for teacher professional development. It was an answer to the question: how do you get new strategies into teachers' pedagogical repertoire. For years it has been known that the one-and-done, after-school in-services are ineffective methods for inducing change or to getting new teaching strategies into classrooms. Instead, teachers need to be introduced to a few strategies over time. They also need to talk and plan with other teachers. Then, they need to try these new strategies, reflect, get feedback, and make the necessary changes. This is the most effective way to introduce new pedagogical strategies into classrooms. This book is designed to be used in this way.

The book describes a variety of basic and advanced teaching strategies. If you are a practicing teacher, you may have encountered some of these strategies during your teacher preparation programs; however, here they were learned largely out of context. Now that you are in an authentic teaching context, you are ready to learn them at deeper levels and apply them directly to your teaching situation.

If you are a preservice teacher encountering these strategies for the first time, do not expect complete mastery. Mastery of any skill occurs over time through repeated practice and exposure. However, this book is written so that you can grasp the essence of these strategies and begin using them immediately in field experiences and in your first year as a classroom teacher.

If you are reading the electronic version of this book, links to short videos describing these strategies have been attached to the end of each chapter. If you are reading a paper version of this book, I have put these video links on my website. They are free and available for anybody to use any time for any purpose.

www.OPDT-Johnson.com

Introduction

How to Use This Book

This book is designed to be a professional development tool for both pre-service and practicing teachers. It provides descriptions, explanations, and examples of a variety of research-based teaching strategies that will enhance your ability to teach effectively. These strategies are appropriate for all teachers (general education, special education, and content area specialists) at all levels (kindergarten through graduate school).

PRESERVICE TEACHERS

If you are currently in a teacher preparation program, do not expect to master the strategies described in this book in a single semester. Mastery of any skill occurs over time through continued exposure and practice. Instead, begin to identify the strategies that you see yourself using. Once you are teaching, you will see how they connect to your particular teaching goals. Then, you will be able to experiment with them in an authentic teaching context and eventually achieve mastery.

PRACTICING TEACHERS

If you are a practicing teacher using this book to enhance your pedagogical repertoire, I recommend that this book be used as part of a study group if possible. (If a study group is unavailable, I have set up a blog on my website for you to use to connect with other teachers.) Focus on one strategy at a time. Meet before implementation to share thoughts for how the strategy might be used. With any strategy, you will need to adopt and adapt it to meet the particular needs of your teaching situation and your teaching style. Then, implement the new strategy. Give yourself a minimum of two weeks to try it out in a variety of teaching situations. Finally, meet back with your group to share your results. The form in textbox Intro 1 can be used to provide structure here. At these meetings, it is common to generate additional ideas for using the new strategy. At this point, you can continue to refine and implement this strategy or move on to another.

Participant:
Strategy:
Date/s of implementation:

1. How did you use the strategy?
2. What seemed to work well?
3. What would you do differently?
4. General observations and analysis:

Textbox Intro 1

The Most Significant Variable

What do you suppose is the most significant variable in determining how much learning goes on in a school or classroom? What do you think has the greatest effect on the quality of education students receive? It is the teacher. Teachers are the most significant variable in determining the quality of education (Darling-Hammond, 1999; Darling-Hammond, Holtzman, Gatlin, & Heilig, 2005; Darling-Hammond & Youngs, 2002; Marzano, Pickering, & Pollock, 2001). So it stands to reason then that one of the most effective ways to improve education is to attract intelligent, creative, innovative, caring, dedicated, and hardworking people into the field and to give them the knowledge and skills necessary to succeed. And this is where you come in.

Part I

PLANNING AND REFLECTING

All teaching strategies are found within the context of a lesson. In this section, two aspects of lesson planning are examined: chapter 1 describes six different lesson plan formats. Chapter 2 describes four essential elements of teaching: knowing, planning, doing, and reflecting with an emphasis on teacher reflection.

Chapter 1

Six Lesson Formats

PLANNING THE LEARNING EXPERIENCE

Effective learning experiences must be planned. Planning is important for three reasons:

• **Thoughtful planning creates more purposeful instruction**. Lesson planning is what links the curriculum to the particulars of instruction. Thoughtful planning also helps you understand the content of the lesson, creates a logical sequence of instructional events, and links activities to instructional objectives.

• **Thoughtful planning enhances learning**. Well-designed lessons increase time on task and help students perceive the structure of new information so they can more easily assimilate it. Planning also affects classroom management by reducing chaos, guiding the flow of events, and keeping students interested and engaged.

• **Thoughtful planning enhances your teaching effectiveness**. Planning enables you to incorporate new instructional strategies and use more complex learning activities.

The Lesson Plan

A lesson plan is a tool to enhance your ability to design learning experiences. A lesson plan organizes your thinking as you put the lesson together and guides your thinking during implementation. If you are a beginning teacher, your lesson plans should be fairly descriptive with all discussion questions listed and the activities clearly explained. This level of planning invites you to think through the entire lesson and thus makes it more likely that your

lesson will be successful. As you become more experienced, the thinking and
planning process becomes internalized and your lessons will need less detail.

SIX LESSON PLAN FORMATS

A single lesson plan format could not possibly fit all the varieties of lessons
that occur in classrooms. Different types of lessons call for different types of
lesson plan formats. Described ahead are lesson plan formats for six distinctly
different types of learning experiences.

Basic Lesson Plan Format

Textbox 1.1 contains the most basic of lesson plan formats. This lesson plan
format is used to provide an organized body of knowledge in a way that
enables learners to assimilate and encode this new information (see chapter 4).

I. Lesson Purpose Statement:

1. A one-sentence statement
   a. describes what you want students to learn or know
2. Example: Students will learn about [*insert topic here*].

II. Input:

1. Specific information you want students to know
2. Use list or outline form
   a. enables you to see structure and sequence
3. Sometimes Input and Activity sections are combined
   a. input, an activity, more input, another activity, etc.

III. Activity:

1. Activities are used to get students to manipulate information from Input
   a. chance to practice learning
2. Used to apply or extend information from the Input
3. Many teaching strategies described in this book can be used here

---

Textbox 1.1 Basic lesson plan

Concept Lesson Plan Format

A concept is a mental abstraction of a category. The salient elements for teaching here are shown in textbox 1.2. They include describing the defining attributes of the concept and showing examples and nonexamples (see chapter 6). At the end of the lesson, students should be able to distinguish between examples and nonexamples of the concept.

I. Learning Purpose Statement:

1. The concept you want students to learn about
2. Example: Students will learn about [*insert concept here*].

II. Input: (Include what students need to know to achieve your purpose statement.)

1. Define the concept
2. Define the attributes
3. Provide examples
   a. examples and nonexamples
4. Guided practice
   a. students practice identifying examples and nonexamples
   b. use as a form of informal assessment

III. Activity/Independent Practice:

1. Used to reinforce, extend, practice, or apply their concept learning
2. Use or apply the concept in some fashion

Textbox 1.2 Concept lesson plan

Skills Lesson Plan Format

Teaching a skill is different from teaching a concept or body of knowledge (see chapter 7). The skills lesson plan format in textbox 1.3 is based on the elements of effective skills instruction. The most important part of this lesson is guided practice where scaffolding takes place. Most lesson formats include only a purpose statement; however, a behavioral objective is preferred by some here with a skills lesson plan format (this will be described further in more detail).

I. Lesson Plan Purpose Statement:

1. The skill you want students to learn or be able to do
2. Example: Students will learn how to [*insert skill here*].

II. Behavioral Objective

1. Optional
2. Describe the behavior you want to see at the end of the lesson
3. Examples:
   a. Students will be able to [*insert skill here*].
   b. Students will demonstrate their learning by [*insert skill here*].

III. Input:

1. Exactly what students need to know in order to perform the skill
2. Identify procedural components—introduce the skill and the specific steps
3. Direct instruction—tell how/why the skill is used
4. Model the use of the skill

IV. Guided Practice (Scaffolded Instruction):

1. Take students through each step of the skill several times
2. Practice with scaffold
   a. students practice using skill with scaffold
   b. gradual release of teacher responsibility
   c. use as a form of informal assessment

V. Activity/Independent Practice:

1. Independent practice of the skill students have just learned
   a. use or apply the skill
2. The goal is practice (not measurement or evaluation)
3. Students should be able to complete with 95 percent to 100 percent success ratio

---

Textbox 1.3 Skills Lesson Plan

Discovery Lesson Plan Format

Discovery learning used inductive reasoning during the initial phases of the lesson (see chapter 8). Textbox 1.4 includes the format used for this type of lesson.

I. Purpose Statement:

1. The concept, topic, or skill you want students to learn
2. Example: Students will learn about/how to [*insert concept, topic, or skill here*].

II. Discovery Activity:

1. Identify elements you want students to discover
2. Design discovery activity that enables discovery of some or all of these elements
3. After discovery activity, students are asked to identify or describe salient elements

III. Input:

1. Students are provided specific information related to lesson purpose
2. Input is used to fill in the blanks or extend initial discoveries

IV. Activity/Independent Practice:

1. Used to reinforce, extend, practice, or apply their learning
2. Use or apply the concept, topic, or skill in some fashion

Textbox 1.4 Discovery Lesson Plan

SRE Lesson Plan Format

The scaffolded reading experience (SRE) lesson plan is used to design experiences that enable students to read text independently (see chapter 23). Textbox 1.5 includes a pre-reading activity that acts as a scaffold to provide the support for reading the upcoming selection. The during-reading activity describes how students will read or encounter the text. The post-reading activity describes how students will interact with the content found in the text.

I. Purpose Statement:

1. Example narrative text: Students will read and enjoy [*insert story or chapter title here*]
2. Example expository text: Students will read and understand [*insert book or chapter title here*]

II. Pre-Reading Activity:

1. Gets students ready to read the text independently
2. 1–4 minutes in duration
3. A link is made to upcoming selection

III. During Reading:

1. Describe exactly how students will read
   a. no round robin reading, popcorn reading

IV. Post-Reading Activity:

1. Invites students to manipulate or become engaged with an idea from the text
2. Narrative texts require aesthetic response activities

Textbox 1.5 SRE Reading Lesson Plan

Writing Lesson Plan Format

The writing lesson plan is based on the five-step writing process: (a) pre-writing, (b) drafting, (c) revising, (d) editing, and (e) sharing (see chapter 24). The lesson plan format in textbox 1.6 shows that this format focuses on the first two steps (pre-writing and drafting), and the last (sharing). It is assumed that students put their drafts in a folder and then select the drafts they wish to take to the revising and editing stages.

I. Purpose:

1. The students will write
2. The students will write about [*insert topic or prompt here*]

II. pre-writing Activity:

1. A strategy to generate or organize ideas

III. During Writing:

1. Students write (5–20 minutes)
2. Initial attempt to get ideas on paper
   a. draft or sloppy copy
   b. do not edit, very little revising

IV. Post-writing/Sharing:

1. Students share:
   a. pairs, small groups, large group, other
2. Students put their drafts in their folders

Textbox 1.6 Writing Lesson Plan

KEEP IT SIMPLE

Keep it simple. Rigor is different from complexity. When lesson plan formats become too complex, there is a tendency to focus on form over function. There are, however, two lesson plan elements of which there are varying perspectives and that warrant a bit more attention: (a) the purpose statement or learning objectives and (b) the place of assessment in a lesson plan. These will be examined here.

A Clearly Defined Purpose or Objective

Regardless of the format, all lesson plans begin with a clearly defined purpose or objective that defines the learning experience and provides focus for your lesson. This means that you are not simply designing an interesting experience or creating a fun activity; rather, you are planning a purposeful learning experience to teach specific skills, concepts, or content. But the question is, should you use a purpose statement? A learning objective? Or both?

• **Purpose statements.** Purpose statements (sometimes referred to as cognitive learning objectives) are in alignment with cognitive psychology. Using a purpose statement, you start here with a very simple question, "What is the purpose of this lesson?" This is answered by a purpose statement: "Students will learn how to/about . . ." A purpose statement then is a single sentence that defines what you want students to learn (see textbox 1.7).

- Students will learn about Hmong cultures.
- Students will learn about the origin of Blue Earth County.
- Students will learn about amphibians.
- Student will learn about the local government: mayor, village board, city officials, and elections.
- Students will learn about classical conditioning.
- Students will learn about lesson planning.
- Students will learn about verbs.

Textbox 1.7 Examples of purpose statements

• **Behavioral objectives.** Behavioral learning objectives are in alignment with behavioral psychology. A behavioral learning objective is a single sentence that defines learning in terms of a behavior you would like to see as a result of instruction (see textbox 1.8). Here, you should be able to say yes or no in terms of if that learning behavior was observed.

- Students will create a Venn diagram to illustrate similarities and differences between Hmong cultures and their own culture.
- Students will create a time line to show seven important events in the origin of Blue Earth County.
- Students will demonstrate their knowledge of amphibians by successfully completing the amphibian worksheet.
- Students will demonstrate their knowledge of local government by successfully completing the government worksheet.
- Students will identify and describe the essential elements of classical conditioning.
- Students will be able to design a simple schema-building lesson plan.
- Students will be able to correctly identify the verbs used in their daily writing sample.

Textbox 1.8 Examples of behavioral objectives

The purpose statement is recommended here for use in most teaching situations because it seems to replicate the type of thinking most successful teachers use when planning lessons. It also keeps the focus on students' learning. Regardless of which is used, everything that follows should support the purpose statement or the behavioral objective. If it does not support it, do not include it.

Assessment Is Optional

Some approaches to lesson planning include a plan for assessment. This element is a description of how students will demonstrate their learning or how it will be determined if the behavioral objective has been met.

Example of a plan for assessment

- **Purpose Statement**: Students will learn about amphibians.
- **Behavioral Objective**: Students will demonstrate their knowledge of amphibians by successfully completing the amphibian worksheet.
- **Assessment:** After the lesson, students will be given a worksheet that addresses nine essential elements from the lesson. Students will work in small groups of three to identify the answers for each.

Textbox 1.9

Keep in mind that learning of any kind is seldom complete after a single encounter with any skill or concept. Instead, students need time to review, reengage, reflect, and manipulate new skills or concepts over time before they are fully learned. Thus, it is recommended that this element not be included in a lesson plan. A more effective approach to assessment is to collect small bits of meaningful data at specific places in the curriculum to see what, if, and to what degree learning is taking place. In this way, assessment is like taking soils samples: You do not dig up the entire lawn to see what kind of soil you have. Instead, you take small samples from different parts of the lawn. Also, assessment involves teacher reflection. This then is the topic of the next chapter.

Chapter 2

The Reflective Teacher

THE PROCESS OF EFFECTIVE TEACHING

Effective teaching is a process involving four separate but complimentary components: knowing, planning, doing, and reflecting.

• **Knowing**. Effective teachers have an organized body of knowledge related to teaching and learning as well as the content areas being taught (Darling-Hammond, 1999; Sternberg & Williams, 2010). This organized body of knowledge enables them to align the approaches and strategies used with a body of research and to make decisions that are more likely to enhance your students' learning.
• **Planning**. Effective teachers plan their learning experiences (see chapter 1). They decide exactly what they want students to learn, the teaching strategies they will use, the questions they may ask, and related activities and assignments. As described in the last chapter, planning enables teachers to create more purposeful and effective instruction and results in fewer behavior management issues.
• **Doing**. This third component involves the actually teaching of the lesson. Here the material to be learned is presented using a variety of research-based methodologies and teaching strategies. This component is the focus of this current book.
• **Reflecting**. What separates effective teachers from those with "growth potential" is the propensity to reflect (Sternberg & Williams, 2010; Zeichner & Liston, 1996). This will be the focus further.

REFLECTION

Effective teachers are reflective teachers. Reflection occurs during the teaching episode in what might be called formative reflection. As well, it occurs after the teaching episode in what might be called summative reflection. Reflective thinking occurs on four levels:

Level 1: Teaching Effectiveness

Effective teachers reflect to assess outcomes as well as to establish failure (Porter, Youngs, & Odden, 2001; Sadker, Sadker, & Zittleman, 2008). They examine the lesson in order to identify those things that worked well and those things that could be done differently. They ask questions such as How did it go? Was I effective in getting ideas across? Did learning taking place? Were students able to take away something of importance? Were students able to construction new knowledge? Is there anything I could change or do better? What worked? Did students learn? Did I achieve my purpose or learning objective? What could I have done differently to make the lesson better or more interesting? Was I successful in differentiating the lesson?

Level 2: Research, Research-Based Practices, or Research-Based Theories

Decisions made by accomplished teachers are grounded in established theory and research-based practices (Porter, Youngs, & Odden, 2001). Reflective teachers pause to examine their teaching practice to see if what they are doing aligns with what they know about teaching and learning. They ask questions such as: Does this align with research-based theory? Can it be supported by one of the learning theories? Does it reflect best practice? Can I find research or research-based theory to support what I am doing? What does the professional literature say about this practice?

Here too you can see the importance of having a sufficient knowledge base in each of the four types of teacher knowledge described in the Introduction of this book: (a) pedagogical knowledge, (b) pedagogical content knowledge, (c) knowledge of content, and (d) knowledge of learners and learning. It is hard to reflect at this level if you have nothing upon which to reflect.

Level 3: Values and Philosophy

Reflective teachers pause to consider if what they are doing is in harmony with their personal and professional values and your philosophy. Questions here include things such as: Does this practice reflect what I value? Am

I practicing what I preach in regard to what I believe to be the purpose of education? Is what I am doing consistent with my teaching philosophy? Is this the type of teacher I am or want to be? Do I value what I am doing?

Teacher reflection at this level is based on the premise that you are able to identify a set of values and a teaching philosophy. A philosophy is a set of principles based on one's values and beliefs that are used to guide one's behavior. In education, a teaching philosophy defines the types of learning experience you value or find of import. It might also identify the type of teacher dispositions or characteristic that you value. Appendix A contains an outline to enable you to begin to define your educational philosophy.

Level 4: Interpersonal and Transpersonal Connections

This fourth level tends to be somewhat esoteric. Reflection at this level is often tied in with one's metaphysical paradigm. It may not be appropriate for all teachers. Here you seek a larger purpose for what you do and your daily lessons. Questions to ask include the following: What does the experience mean? Where does it bring you? How are you connecting with something beyond yourself? What is the lesson beyond the lesson? What is the larger human dimension? What is the emotional and intuitive impact? Who am I? What am I learning?

FINAL WORD

All teachers have lessons or parts of lessons that are unsuccessful or do not go as planned. The difference between an effective teacher and a teacher with "growth potential" is that the effective teacher reflects to see what could have been done differently. The teacher with "growth potential" will not. Effective teachers are reflective teachers. Continued growth and evolution as a teacher is impossible without some sort of reflection.

Part II

TEACHER-CENTERED INSTRUCTION

This section focuses on *teacher-centered* instructional strategies. With this type of strategy, the teacher is primarily responsible for transmitting knowledge directly to the students in a very controlled, sequential manner (Borich, 2006; Kauchak & Eggen, 2001). There are four types of teacher-centered instructional strategies described here: (a) direction instruction, (b) expository teaching, (c) direction instruction for teaching concepts, and (d) direct instruction for teaching skills.

MODELS, METHODS, AND STRATEGIES

Sometimes the strategies described in this section are referred to as instructional models or methods; however, this these terms are not accurate in this context. An *instructional model* is a defined way of teaching that involves specific steps and a set of procedures that can be applied to many subject areas. An *instructional method* or (method of instruction) usually refers to a specific set of techniques that are used in a prescribed fashion for instruction in a specific subject area (e.g., math methods and reading methods). However, one of the limitations of instructional models and methods is that there is no singular one that works best for all students all the time. The students in your classes are not standardized educational products and you are not a standardized teaching machine. One type of instruction does not work for all.

Therefore, even though this section contains what is often called both models and methods of instruction, they are strategies that should be considered. An *instructional strategy* (or pedagogical strategy) is a specific technique that is used selectively for a specific purpose at specific times. This distinction is important because each strategy is useful in some places with some students, but not in others. Each strategy should be adopted and adapted to meet the needs of the students with whom you are working as well as to achieve the specific purpose of the lesson. None of the instructional strategies described in this book (or any book) should ever be used as the sole means of instruction. To do so is to reduce teaching to a formula.

An analogy is this: a teaching strategy is like a golf club. A driver is a very effective golf club to use when you want the ball to travel a long distance, but not if you are in a sand trap or close to the green. Thus, master golfers, like master teachers, do not carry a single club; rather, a set of clubs because their golf ball lands in all sorts of places. No teacher should be equipped with a single model or method. Instead, teachers should have many strategies.

Chapter 3

Direct Instruction

Direct instruction is a pedagogical strategy with which all teachers should be familiar. It is defined that here is structured form of teaching in which students receive information directly from a teacher (Ormrod, 2006). The responsibility for students' learning rests firmly on the teacher. The teacher sets the purpose for the lesson, explains exactly what the students are to learn, and evaluates learning based on students' ability to represent or replicate predetermined knowledge or skills.

DIRECT INSTRUCTION COMPONENTS

There are a variety of forms of direct instruction each of which includes some or all of the following seven components described here:

1. **Clearly defined purpose or objective.** As described in chapter 1, this enables you to plan a purposeful learning experience to teach a specific body of knowledge or a specific skill.

2. **Overview.** The overview occurs during the initial part of a direct instruction lesson. Here, the teacher tells students exactly what the lesson objective is and presents an overview or preview of what is to come. This provides learners with the big picture so that they can contextualize the information to come. In other words, seeing the structure of what is to be learned (the big picture) helps students process and encode new information. This usually involves presenting some form of an advanced organizer (chapter 4). The overview part of direct instruction should be kept relatively brief (from one to three minutes in duration).

3. **Input.** The input is the specific information that you want students to know. If you are presenting topical information (declarative knowledge), include all the information that students need to know and the sequence in which it is presented (see chapter 4). If you are teaching a skill (procedural knowledge), include a description of the skill, how to use it, the specific steps, and examples or modeling (see chapter 7). In each situation, the input for a direct instruction lesson should be well organized with a logical structure to enhance students' ability to assimilate and encode this new information. This again points to the importance of thoughtful planning.

4. **Guided practice.** Guided practice is an experience in which students practice the skill or manipulate content with some sort of scaffold. A scaffold in education is a type of structure or support that enables all students to be successful during the initial phases of learning. The goal here is for students to use, apply, practice, or try out new content as the teacher monitors to assess learning (formative assessment). Small group activities are often used here because they enable the teacher to observe many students simultaneous and hear their thought processes as they discuss ideas with others.

When teaching a skill, guided practice involves the teacher taking the class through each step the skill together with a gradual release of responsibility (see chapter 7). This means that the first attempts are done together in a large group, the next are done in a small group or with a partner, and the last are done individually so that the teacher has a good sense of students' level of success. This last step enables the teacher to go back and reteach elements as necessary.

5. **Independent practice.** Independent practice is the application of what students have learned. Here you want students to apply or extend the new knowledge or skill in some way. This is not the place to assess learning (although it is often used for this); rather, the intent is for students to practice what they have already learned.

6. **Revisit, review, and reapply.** As stated previously, mastery of anything does not occur in a single encounter. Learners must revisit and reapply concepts and skills for learning to become more complete. For mastery to occur, students need to encounter concepts and skills many times, over time, and in a variety of situations and settings.

FINAL WORD

Described here are some of the basic elements of direct instruction. However, not all elements need to be included when using direct instruction. As well, direct instruction, like each strategy described in this book, is a tool. Like any tool, its effectiveness is determined by how it is used. Direct instruction is most effective when it is used as one of many pedagogical strategies that is flexibly applied as needed.

Chapter 4

Expository Teaching, Meaningful Learning, and Schema-Building Lessons

BUILDING, EXPANDING, AND REARRANGING SCHEMATA

Expository teaching is a form of direct instruction that involves using a lecture, presentation, or some form of telling strategy to provide the information students need to know in a clear and purposeful way (Woolfolk, 2007). It is based on the idea that well-presented input (lecture) can be an effective form of teaching with students at any age and level if the material being presented is organized, well planned, and connected to prior knowledge. This chapter describes expository teaching and puts it in the context of a schema-building lesson.

Schema and Schemata

The schema-building lesson has its origin in cognitive psychology. Here, learning is viewed as a change in cognitive structures. A cognitive structure is like a file folder in your head used to organize bodies of information. Within this file cabinet are the individual file folders related to specific bodies of information called schema or schemata (plural). We can say that learning has occurred when new file folders (schemata) are added into the file cabinet or when the file folders are expanded or rearranged to accommodate new information. The purpose then of the schema-building lesson is to build or expand upon students' declarative knowledge base.

Meaningful Learning

The goal of expository teaching is *meaningful learning*. This is when new information connects to or builds upon what students already know (Ormrod,

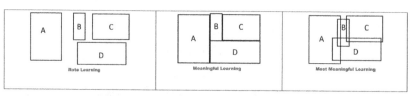

Figure 4.1   Rote, meaningful, and most meaningful learning

2012). The opposite of meaningful learning is *rote learning*. This is when new information is taken in, but it is not connected to anything known (see figure 4.1). For example, if you memorized a list of terms without knowing what they meant, this would be rote learning. It would be very hard to use this information and this information would be easily forgotten. But if you could connect these same terms to things you already knew and understood, this would be meaningful learning. It could be used to understand new ideas and it would be more easily retained in memory than would disconnected information.

A third term, *most meaningful learning*, is when you can show the interconnectedness of things. This is not just showing how things are related, but going beyond and showing how they are interrelated or part of the same larger system. That is, they are essentially the same. This concept may be a bit esoteric and you may not see the application to your current teaching situation, but this is the ultimate type of teaching and learning.

So, how do you design lessons that develop meaningful and not rote learning? First, make sure the material to be learned is organized and presented in ways that students can easily understand. This includes using "kid language" and not "dictionary language" in your explanations. Second, design activities that enable students to be actively engaged with the material they are learning. And third, make connections from the new material to students' lives, experiences, or prior knowledge.

Advance Organizers

Advanced organizers can be used to make connections and organize new information before the lesson. An advance organizer is any form of visual, verbal, or written material that depicts the content to be learned (Mayer & Wittrock, 2006). It provides a very general sense of the overall structure of the information to be presented in the upcoming lesson. According to David Ausubel (1977), the advance organizer has three main purposes:

• **Highlight key points**. Advance organizers can be used to direct students' attention to the important parts of the upcoming lesson. This gives

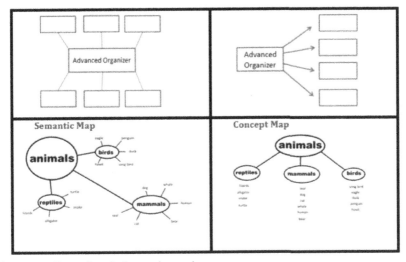

Figure 4.2   Examples of advanced organizers

students the big picture and enables them to put new facts and concepts in a meaningful context.

• **Activate relevant knowledge**. Advance organizers can also be used to remind students of the relevant knowledge they already know. This helps students make the connections between the known and the new.

• **Show relationships**. Finally, advance organizers can be used to show the relationship between important points described in the upcoming input. Put another way, advanced organizers are designed to show students the superordinate, ordinate, and subordinate relationship between key concepts.

Advance organizers take a variety of forms including: (a) an outline; (b) a quick verbal overview that identifies the main points to be learned; (c) a picture or graphic that shows the concept's ordinate, superordinate, and subordinate parts; (d) a semantic map or concept map, (e) concrete models; (f) analogies; a discussion of the main themes or ideas; (g) a set of defining attributes or higher order rules; (h) Venn diagrams or comparison charts, and (i) a short abstract or summary of material to be learned or read. To be effective, learners should be able to clearly see the structure of the material to be learned. Figure 4.2 shows examples of some common types of advanced organizers.

USING A SCHEMA-BUILDING LESSON PLAN FOR EXPOSITORY TEACHING

In this section, the elements of expository teaching are put in the context of a schema-building lesson plan. Schema-building lessons are used to develop declarative knowledge (versus procedural knowledge). If you are a preservice or beginning teacher, you may be required to design lessons that include all these parts. For experienced teachers, it is recommended that you adopt and adapt as needed. Note the similarities between the direct instruction and schema-building lessons in table 4.1. The biggest difference is that the direct instruction lesson plan can be used to teach both declarative and procedural knowledge (a skill). The schema-building lesson plan is used just for teaching declarative knowledge.

Elements of a Schema-Building Lesson Plan

• **Academic standard(s) (if applicable).** An academic standard defines the knowledge and skills that students are expected to learning in a subject area. It could be a curriculum standard, a content standard (math, social studies, reading, music, etc.), or a state or national academic standard such as one from the Common Core State Standards (CCSS) (see textbox 4.1). Thus said, not all lessons are based on specific academic standards.

Table 4.1   Comparison of direct instruction and schema-building lessons

Direct Instruction Lesson	Schema-Building Lesson
1. Purpose or objective	1. Academic standard(s)
2. Overview	2. Purpose or objective
3. Input	3. Opening/overview
4. Guided practice	4. Input
5. Questions/probing	5. Independent practice or
6. Independent practice	activity
7. Revisit, review, and reapply	6. Reflection

CCSS.ELA-LITERACY

Explain major differences between poems, drama, and prose, and refer to the structural elements of poems (e.g., verse, rhythm, and meter) and drama (e.g., casts of characters, settings, descriptions, dialogue, and stage directions) when writing or speaking about a text.

Textbox 4.1   4th grade common core state standard related to literacy

Rarely do you address an entire academic standard in one lesson or setting. Thus, purpose statements usually involve one aspect of an academic standard. For example, textbox 4.1 contains a 4th grade CCSS standard related to literacy. The standard provides guidance for a curriculum. However, to adequately address this standard, you would need to teach a variety of lessons related to poetry, drama, and prose. In each lesson, you would teach students about the structural elements of each.

• **Purpose statement or behavioral objective**. Purpose statements and behavioral objectives have been described previously.

• **Overview**. This has been described earlier. Again, it should be relatively short, generally lasting between thirty seconds to three minutes. This is where the advanced organizer is used. The purpose is to connect the new information to what students might already know, and to provide an overview of the lesson. This should be short and briskly paced.

• **Input**. This is the heart of the schema-building lesson. Here you present the specific information that students need for learning to occur. This is presented in an organized fashion so that students can easily encode this new material. It is recommended that you use an outline or a list form with short abbreviated sentences for your lesson plan. This will enable you to quickly see the structure and sequence of the input as you teach so that you can teach from the lesson without reading directly from it.

Example:

1. Use short, abbreviated sentences for input
   a. Enables you to quickly see structure
   b. Can better organize
   c. Can teach from outline without reading

2. Include questions for discussion
   a. Q: How should they be represented?
   b. Use simple /Q/
   c. Good discussions are planned

3. Include teacher directions
   a. [ask students to turn to neighbor here]

Textbox 4.2

• **Independent practice or activity.** This is where students practice what they have just learned in your lesson. If you have done your job, students should be able to do this with 95 percent to 100 percent success. The big idea here is that this is a practice of what students have already learned. It should be designed to practice or reinforce learning. The purpose of this element is NOT to measure, evaluate, or challenge students. It is to practice learning. Although this can be used as a form of assessment, it does not have to be so. Many of the strategies described in this book can be designed for use here.

• **Reflection.** Reflection is an important part of teaching. It is what enables you to continue to grow and evolve as a teacher. You should ask some or all of the following types of questions: Did students learn? What part of the lesson seemed to be successful? What could I change or do differently next time to make the lesson more effective? Based on today's lesson, what should I reteach or review? Based on today's lesson what should I teach next? Does the lesson align with my values and teaching philosophy? Does the lesson align with a body of research or research-based theory?

FINAL WORD

The goal of expository teaching is to help students construct knowledge and to develop or expand their knowledge base. Regardless of what your teaching philosophy is or which teaching strategies you favor, being able to present information clearly in ways that students can understand is a necessary skill.

Chapter 5

The Process of Planning
a Schema-Building Lesson

THE PROCESS

In regards to lesson planning, often the only thing considered is what the final product should look like or what should be contained in each of the lesson plan parts. This chapter will examine the process used to move from an academic standard to purpose statement, objective, assessment, lesson input, and activity for a schema-building lesson plan. Once you understand the process, designing the product becomes easier.

Step 1: Analyze the Academic Standards

Many of the lesson plan formats require teachers to include an academic standard (see chapter 4). Textbox 5.1 contains an example of a 3rd grade academic standard from the Minnesota Academic Standards for Science K–12 and a suggested benchmark (http://education.state.mn.us/MDE/dse/stds/). A *benchmark* in education is some type of product, performance, or assessment used to determine if students have met a standard or set of standards. Note that the benchmark included with this standard is a suggested benchmark. It describes one method that could be used to enable students to demonstrate their learning. Other methods can also be used.

- **Academic Standard (Life Science):** Structure and Function of Living Systems. Understand that living things are diverse with many different characteristics that enable them to grow, reproduce, and survive.
  Suggested benchmark: Sort animals into groups, such as mammals and amphibians, based on physical characteristics.

Textbox 5.1 Example of an academic standard

A distinction needs to be made between academic standards and curriculums: an academic defines in a general sense the knowledge and skills to be learned. Academic standards are used to inform curriculums (curricula), but they technically are not a curriculum. A *curriculum* is a systematic plan for instruction designed by teachers within a school district or at various grade levels for each subject area. It describes what specific knowledge and skills are taught, in what general order, and in what context. Curriculums are usually designed by teachers based on their (a) knowledge of the content, (b) knowledge of students' developmental levels, interests, and needs; and (c) pedagogical content knowledge [this is the knowledge of how to teach various subject areas]. This points to the need for knowledgeable teachers and the importance of continued professional development (see introduction).

Figure 5.1 shows the relationship between academic standards, teachers, curriculums, and lessons.

Step 2: Decide What to Teach

Planning a curriculum is beyond the scope of this current book; however, the next step in designing an individual lesson is to decide what to teach. Note that the standard related to Life Science in textbox 5.1 is a superordinate category; not a topic. It provides guidance for the inclusion of several possible topics and skills within the curriculum. The specific topics and related content for the lesson should come from a curriculum.

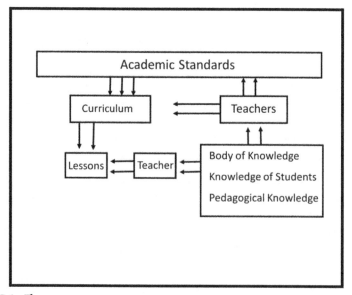

Figure 5.1   The process

It is common that a curriculum guide or teachers' manual will not contain everything you need to teach an effective lesson. This means that you must often do additional research to design a lesson. This involves finding and reading additional material and taking notes. After the information needed to teach the lesson has been gathered, then decide what should be contained in the individual lesson. Start with an outline based on your notes of the previous section. This can be done on a computer or paper and should be apart from any lesson plan format used. This outline enables you to begin seeing the structure and sequence of the information you will provide.

At this point, you have a sense of what you are going to teach, but it still needs to be clarified. During this part of the lesson planning process, you are deciding what students need to know as well as what they can learn in a single learning experience. Keep in mind that dumping more information on students does not mean that more learning will take place. Providing too much information can be just as confusing as providing too little information. You must also decide how and in what order the information will be presented.

Step 3: Identify the Purpose Statement

Now you should be able to create the *purpose statement*. As described in chapter 4, this is a one-sentence statement that describes exactly what it is you want students to learn or learn about (see textbox 5.2). You are probably beginning to see that lesson planning is not a linear process moving neatly from one step to another in an orderly fashion. It is a recursive process in which each subsequent part of the lesson may inform a previous part. It is common to find yourself going back to change something you have already written based on what you are currently writing.

- **Academic Standard (Life Science):** Structure and Function of Living Systems. Understand that living things are diverse with many different characteristics that enable them to grow, reproduce, and survive.
  Suggested benchmark: Sort animals into groups, such as mammals and amphibians, based on physical characteristics.
- **Purpose Statement:** Students will learn about amphibians.

Textbox 5.2 Academic standards, benchmarks and purpose standards

Step 4: Design the Behavioral Objective

If a behavioral objective is used (which is not always the case), the next step is to describe learning in terms of a behavior that you would like to see at the end of the lesson. That is, if students have learned the content in a meaning-ful way, what will they be able to do? What behavior will demonstrate their learning? How might they use, apply, reflect, or describe their new learning?

Behavioral objectives come in a variety of forms ranging from general to very precise. For example, the behavioral objective in textbox 5.3 indicates that students will be able to complete a worksheet. This is an example of a general behavioral objective. It does not indicate whether students will com-plete the worksheet as part of that day's lesson or on another day. Neither does it describe the specific criteria necessary for success. And, it does not indicate the content of the worksheet other than something related to amphib-ians. It simply says that at some point, students will complete a worksheet, it will be about amphibians, and they will be successful.

- **Academic Standard (Life Science):** Structure and Function of Liv-ing Systems. Understand that living things are diverse with many dif-ferent characteristics that enable them to grow, reproduce, and survive. *Suggested benchmark:* Sort animals into groups, such as mammals and amphibians, based on physical characteristics.
- **Purpose Statement:** Students will learn about amphibians.
- **Behavioral Objective:** Students will demonstrate their knowledge of amphibians by successfully completing 90 percent of the questions on the amphibian worksheet.

Textbox 5.3 Behavioral objectives

The precision of a behavioral objective could be enhanced by providing a general sense of what students are to master. For example: *Students will be able to correctly identify five characteristics of amphibians.* This indicates what the assignment might be, but does not specifically define it. It also leads to input that focuses more specifically on amphibian characteristics. Precise objectives generally result in narrower input when compared to general objectives. However, precise objectives do not always result in more learn-ing. One is not more effective than the other; rather, different types of input and activity are used to support different types of objectives.

The behavioral objective often points to an assignment or activity that will occur at the end of the lesson as in the following: *Students will create a Venn diagram comparing and contrasting reptiles and amphibians.* This tells me that the assignment or activity will involve the creation of a Venn diagram, but it does not define it in terms of what the criteria for success might be. Instruction here would focus on amphibian characteristics with a review of reptile character-istics from a previous lesson. However, with this objective, there is no criterion for success, simple that students will do this. The objective could be clarified and made more precise by stating: *Students will use a Venn diagram to identify at least three similarities and three differences between reptiles and amphibians.*

The behavioral objective could also be specifically related to the assessment. For example: *Students will score 90 percent or more on the postlesson amphibian quiz.* Using an assessment-related behavioral objective such as this, the lesson focus becomes on meeting that specific behavioral objective. The salient idea here is that the type of objective used greatly influences the input and activity that follow. As you can see, things can get a bit muddled in the land of behavioral objectives.

Step 5: Identify and Plan the Assessment

As stated in a previous chapter, not every lesson needs to be assessed. In fact, much of what we call assessment is, in fact, teacher reflection. And effective teachers do this naturally. There does not need to be a formalized plan. However, if you insist on including a formal assessment plan as part of your schema-building lesson plan, the next step is to figure out how will you know if learning has occurred. Here you will describe both the product and process related to the assessment. If you are using a behavioral objective, this will be your plan for determining whether and to what degree the behavioral objective has been met (see textbox 5.4). If you are using a purpose statement, this will describe how students might demonstrate what they have learned.

In the plan for assessment, this is usually two to six sentences. It is based on the behavioral objective and/or purpose statement and describes exactly how you will assess learning. It is recommended that you create a very flexible first draft here. This is because the assessment and the behavioral objective often change slightly depending on the specific input (information) that you include (see later in this book).

- **Academic Standard (Life Science):** Structure and Function of Living Systems. Understand that living things are diverse with many different characteristics that enable them to grow, reproduce, and survive. *Suggested benchmark:* Sort animals into groups, such as mammals and amphibians, based on physical characteristics.
- **Purpose Statement:** Students will learn about amphibians.
- **Behavioral Objective:** Students will demonstrate their knowledge of amphibians by successfully completing the amphibian worksheet.
- **Assessment:** After the lesson, students will be given a worksheet that addresses nine essential elements from the lesson. Students will work in small groups of three to identify the answers for each.

Textbox 5.4 Assessment

In your lesson, these assessment generally occurs in one of the three ways: (a) during the lesson as you are observing students engaged in a lesson-related activity; (b) after the lesson as an assignment, product, performance, or short measure; or (c) as a more formalized measure or assignment on another day. Keep in mind that assessment does not always have to occur in the same lesson. It could be a part of a unit test or exam (see Textbox 5.5). Thus said, a plan for assessment should be considered optional. At some point, children need to be trusted for their own learning.

Assessment: Students will demonstrate their understanding of amphibians by creating a diagram or sketch that contains each salient characteristic. After the lesson, students will be asked to review each characteristic in a small group. Then individually, they will use poster paper to create a design, diagram, or picture that illustrates the function of each element.

Textbox 5.5 Assessment in the form of an activity

Step 6: Design the Input

Much of the information you want to provide students may already have been determined already as part of Step 2. Your task in this step is to determine exactly what is presented and how it will be presented.

Step 7: Independent Practice or Activity

This is where students practice what they have just learned in your lesson. As described previously, this is practice of what students have already learned. It should be designed to extend, practice, or reinforce learning. Thus said, this can be used as a form of assessment, although it does not have to be so. Your assessment (if you choose to include it) and your independent activity could look very similar.

REFLECTION

As stated previously, reflection is a natural part of effective teaching. Over time, this becomes a natural part of effective teachers' teaching repertoire. You should ask some or all of the following types of questions:

- Did students learn?
- What part of the lesson seemed to be successful?

- What could be changed or done differently next time to make the lesson more effective?
- Based on today's lesson, what needs to be retaught or reviewed?
- Based on today's lesson what should I teach next?
- Does the lesson align with my values and teaching philosophy?
- Does the lesson align with a body of research or research-based theory?

FINAL WORD

Two points to keep in mind as you ponder the process of planning a learning experience: first, keep it simple. Teaching need not be complicated. The essence of teaching, whether at the graduate level or in a kindergarten or preschool is this: say a little bit; do a little bit. With older students, you say a little bit more and do a little bit less. With younger students, you say a little bit less and do a little bit more. And second, effective teaching is not defined by what you say or do; effective teaching is defined by what students learn.

Chapter 6

Using Direct Instruction to Teach Concepts

Much of your teaching life will involve teaching concepts. A *concept* is a unit of thought that organizes ideas or experiences. It is the mental abstraction of a category. For example, the following are concepts: freedom, empathy, interdependence, fairness, triangle, verbs, religion, region, paragraphs, government, justice, democracy, wants and needs, economic system, virtues, values, country, state, values, or environment.

Items within a concept share a set of essential characteristics or defining attributes. *Defining attributes* are the features that make the thing a concept. For example, the defining attributes of a country are (a) it has recognized boundaries or boarders, (b) it has a government that runs the country and provides certain public services such as education and police, (c) it has some sort of economy or system of money, and (d) it has sovereignty or makes decisions from within the country.

Concept learning is being able to recognize valid examples of the concept (Ormrod, 2012). That is, students can discriminate between valid and non-valid examples. To teach concepts using direct instruction use the following steps:

1. **Present a definition of the concept**. Your definition should use words and concepts with which students are familiar. In other words, use "kid language" instead of dictionary language. One rule of defining a concept is that you cannot use the word or a form of the word in the definition.

Ineffective example: Freedom is the ability to be free.
Effective example: Freedom is when you are able to make choices about
    what you want to say or do.

2. **Present defining attributes of the concepts**. Tell students that in order for something to be the concept, it must have all of the defining attributes. *Concepts maps,* sometimes called semantic maps, can be used here (see figure 6.1). These are any type of visual representation of a concept that shows the relationship among ordinate and subordinate parts. Concept maps can be used during the teaching or as postlesson activities.

3. **Present positive examples of the concept.** Students should be given many examples of the concept to be learned. (Think of three as the minimum number of examples you must provide.) With each example, emphasize the defining attributes (tell why the concept is the concept). An *attribute chart* can be used here (see figures 6.2 and 6.3). This is a table that has examples and nonexamples concepts on the vertical axis and the defining attributes along the horizontal axis on top. In order to be the concept, it must have all the attributes.

4. **Present negative examples of the concept.** Students should be given some examples of things that are similar but are not the concept. Use the defining attributes to describe why each example is not the concept. (Remember that all the defining attributes must be present for it to be the concept.)

5. **Use guided practice to identify concepts.** Present both positive and negative examples to students. Ask students to identify each and tell why it is or is not the concept and provide feedback related to their responses. This acts as a type of formative assessment (assessment while learning is still forming) that tells you if you need to reteach any part of the concept lesson.

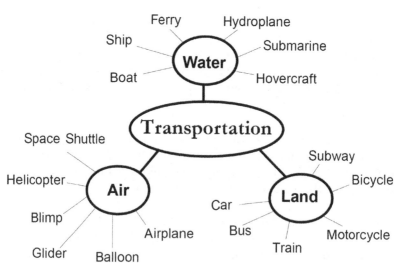

Figure 6.1   Concept map

Concept: A Virtue				
	Personal character trait	Nurtures or helps others	Can't see it	Causes us to act
compassion	x	x	x	x
democracy		x		
capitalism		x		x
honesty	x	x	x	x
anger	x		x	x
fortitude				
rules		x		x
peacefulness	x	x	x	x
competitive	x		x	x

Figure 6.2   Attribute chart for a virtue

Concept: Want vs. Need				
	Can't live without it	Helps us stay alive	Makes our life more enjoyable or better	We touch it every day
TV			x	
food	x	x	x	x
computer			x	
clothes	x	x	x	x
comb			x	x
school			x	
transportation	x	x	x	x

Figure 6.3   Attribute chart for want versus need

6. Use independent practice to reinforce concept learning. Independent practice is any activity that gets students using the concept. Here students practice what they have already learned related to concepts. Independent practice can be done individually or in small groups.

FINAL WORD

The basic lesson plan for using direct instruction to teach concepts is in textbox 6.1. Direct instruction is one of several ways to teach concepts. Discovery learning and inquiry learning can also be used to achieve the same purpose and will be described in later chapters.

I. Learning Purpose Statement:

1. The concept you want students to learn about
2. Example: Students will learn about [*insert concept here*].

II. Input: (Include what students need to know to achieve your purpose statement.)

1. Define the concept
2. Define the attributes
3. Provide examples
   a. examples and nonexamples
4. Guided practice
   a. students practice identifying examples and nonexamples
   b. use as a form of informal assessment

III. Activity/Independent Practice:

1. Used to reinforce, extend, practice, or apply their concept learning
2. Use or apply the concept in some fashion

Textbox 6.1 Concept lesson plan

Chapter 7

Teaching a Skill

Effective teachers in all areas and at all levels use direct and explicit instruction in some form to teach procedural knowledge or skills. However, direct instruction should be thought of as a pedagogical skill, not a method or an approach to teaching any subject. Put another way, it should never be used as the sole form of instruction in any area for any subject. This chapter describes the basic elements necessary to teach a skill of using direct instruction.

THE BASIC ELEMENTS OF SKILLS LESSON PLAN

The elements used to teach a skill presented here are based on the elements of effective skills instruction (Johnson, 2000; Pressley, Harris, & Marks, 1992) and include the following: (a) a purpose or objective; (b) input with the identification of procedural components, modeling, and examples; (c) guided practice; (d) independent practice, and (e) review.

A Clearly Defined Purpose or Objective

As described previously, a clearly defined purpose or objective for a skills lesson describes exactly what you want students to learn how to do. It defines the learning experience and provides focus for your lesson. Here you are not simply designing an interesting experience or creating a fun activity; instead, you are planning a purposeful learning experience to teach or help develop a specific skill. Below are examples of both for a skills lesson plan: purpose statements and behavioral objectives. Regardless of which is used, everything that follows should support it. If it does not support the purpose or objective, do not include it.

Examples of purpose statements

- Students will learn about the short /a/ sound.
- Students will learn how to make story predictions.
- Students will learn about the /sp/ beginning blend.
- Students will learn about question marks.
- Students will learn past, present, and future tense.

Textbox 7.1

Examples of behavioral objectives

- Students will be able to identify words with a short /a/ sound.
- Students will be able to use clues to make story predictions.
- Students will be able to identify words with a /sp/ beginning blend.
- Students will be able to correctly use the question mark as ending punctuation while writing.
- Students will be able to use questions marks to identify questions during reading.
- Students will be able to correctly identify past, present, and future tense.

Textbox 7.2

Input

The input is the specific information that students need to know to be able to perform the skill. Input for a skills lesson plan should be well organized and structured to enhance students' understanding. Using a list or an outline form will enable you to easily see the structure and logical sequence of your input during the planning as well as when you are while teaching. The input should include the following:

• **Identification of the procedural components**. If the skill involves several steps, first introduce the skill by telling what is, what it is used for, and how it is used. Then identify the specific steps of procedural components (see textbox 7.1).

1. This is [insert skill here]
2. It is used for [insert purpose here]
3. These are the steps:
   a.
   b.
   c.

Textbox 7.3 Example input for a reading sub-skill

While some skills, such as like long division, have specific steps, other skills, such as literacy subskills, do not. For example, if you are teaching students to recognize a letter-sound relationship or to identify verbs within a sentence, these are skills without procedural components. We want students to be able to do these, but there are no steps involved. In cases such as these, simply introduce the subskill and provide examples (see textbox 7.2).

---

1. This is the letter a
2. It is a vowel
3. It makes the short /a/ (ah) sound as in:
   a. hat
   b. man
   c. lap

Textbox 7.4 Example input for a reading sub-skill

• **Modeling, demonstration, and/or examples.** Next, model the skill by thinking out loud while going through each step. If it is a reading subskill (such as a letter pattern or sound), provide many examples here. For example, with the short /a/ lesson plan discussed, students would be shown many examples of short /a/ words. They would see them and practice reading through them several times.

Guided Practice

Guided practice, sometimes referred to as *scaffolded instruction*, is the most important component in teaching a skill. Here, the teacher takes students through each step of the skill several times. The goal is to provide the support necessary for them to eventually use the skill independently (Perry, Turner, & Meyer, 2006). Students should use, apply, or practice the skill several times as the teacher monitors their performance to assess learning (formative assessment). Small group activities can be effective here because they enable the teacher to see many students simultaneous and to hear their thought processes as they discuss ideas with others. Guided practice should get students ready to use the skill independently during independent practice.

Independent Practice

Independent practice is used to practice or reinforce the skill taught (see the next section). Students should be able to do this with 95 percent to

100 percent success ratio. Also, even though activities here are often used for assessment, this is not the purpose.

Examples of independent practice

Mr. Burns and questions marks. After a guided practice activity used to help students learn about question marks (discussed previously), Mr. Burns engaged in a large group discussion with his 2nd grade class where they generated questions or things about which they wondered or wanted to learn. In their journals, each student then wrote three questions related to things they wanted to learn.

Ms. Woodson and the short /a/ sound. Ms. Woodson used direct instruction and guided practice to teach her 2nd grade students about the short /a/ sound. Guided practice consisted of students working in pairs to complete a worksheet under her direction. For independent practice, students described something that makes them mad (short /a/ word).

Ms. Jones and multiplying fractions. Ms. Jones used direct instruction and guided practice to teach her students how to multiply fractions. Once she had a sense that her students had learned how to do this, she assigned eight problems from the textbook so students could practice their learning.

Textbox 7.5

Revisit, Review, and Reapply

Even if students demonstrate "mastery" of a behavioral objective, do not assume that mastery has occurred. Mastery of any skill occurs over time as learners encounter a new skill in a variety of situations and settings.

SKILLS LESSON PLAN

The skills lesson plan format in textbox 7.3 was introduced in chapter 1. The following are two examples of skills lesson plans (see textboxes 7.4 and 7.5).

I. Lesson Plan Purpose Statement:

1. The skill you want students to learn or be able to do
2. Example: Students will learn how to [*insert skill here*].

II. Behavioral objective

1. Optional
2. Describe the behavior you want to see at the end of the lesson
3. Examples:
   a. Students will be able to [insert skill here].
   b. Students will demonstrate their learning by [insert skill here].

III. Input:

1. Exactly what students need to know in order to perform the skill
2. Identify procedural components—introduce the skill and the specific steps
3. Direct instruction—tell how/why the skill is used
4. Model the use of the skill

IV. Guided practice (scaffolded instruction):

1. Take students through each step of the skill several times
2. Practice with scaffold
   a. students practice using skill with scaffold
   b. gradual release of teacher responsibility
   c. use as a form of informal assessment

V. Activity/Independent Practice:

1. Independent practice of the skill students have just learned
   a. use or apply the skill
2. The goal is practice (not measurement or evaluation)
3. Students should be able to complete with 95 percent to 100 percent success ratio

Textbox 7.6 Skills lesson plan

PURPOSE STATEMENT: Students will learn about thinking skills.
   OBJECTIVE: Students will use the thinking skill, *Creating Groups* to put current events into categories.
   INTRODUCTION: Boys and girls, today we are going to learn how to use a new thinking skill called creating groups.

INPUT:

1. Thinking skills are the skills we use to help organize our thoughts.
2. They have specific steps to follow.
3. They make complicated thinking seem easy.
4. Creating groups is a thinking skills.
   a. Scientists often use this.
   b. Look at animals, organism, rocks, and so on; look for patterns, and make sense of it by putting in groups (show example with animal pictures).

5. These are the steps:
   a. Look at the whole.
   b. Identify reoccurring themes or patterns.
   c. Arrange into groups or categories.
   d. Describe.

6. Watch me as I do this (show a screen with a variety of animals).
   a. Look at the whole—I am looking at all the animals.
   b. Reoccurring themes—animals with hooves, horns, wings, and so on.
   c. Groups—move each animal into a group.
   d. Describe the animals in terms of the number of groups and the number of animals within each group (use a bar graph).

GUIDED PRACTICE:

1. In large group, brainstorm to list ten interesting events that have happened at school in the last week.
   a. Think aloud (cognitive modeling) to help students organize into groups.
   b. Example: Are there things that are the same here?

2. Describe the whole in terms of groups and numbers within each group.

ACTIVITY:

1. In a small group, students list at least twenty current events that have happened this year.
2. Use Creating Groups to find categories

3. Describe these events in terms of the groups.
   a. What does this tell you about this year?
   b. How does this year compare to last year?

Textbox 7.7 Lesson plan to teach a thinking skill

I. PURPOSE STATEMENT: Students will learn about verbs.

II. INPUT

1. **Ask the class to name some of the things they do after school.**
   a. Examples: reading, running, playing, talking, sleeping, and so on.
   b. Write examples on the board.

2. The things you chose are all verbs!
   a. Verb is an action
   b. A doing word
   c. A thing or person is doing something.

3. Examples (these sentences will be written on the Smart Board):
   a. Milo was drinking milk.
   b. Sally was playing baseball.
   c. The plate fell to the floor.
   d. The dog barked at the cat.

4. These are all actions.
   a. What is Milo doing?
   b. What was sally doing?
   c. What did the plate do?
   d. What did the dog do?

5. Remember, a noun is a thing
   a. person, place, or thing.
   b. you can see it.
   c. you can touch it?
   d. Can you see milk?
   e. Can you see drinking? (No, you can see a person drinking, you can see a person doing an action.)

6. Find the nouns in the sentences (in the previous section).

III. GUIDED PRACTICE

1. [The following sentences will appear individually on the smart board. They are taken from today's story.]
   a. Billy Marbel with Riding on the bus.
   b. He was going to school.
   c. He looked out the window.
   d. A spaceship was flying in the sky.
   e. An alien looked out the window.
   f. The alien waved at Billy.

2. The first two sentences (a and b)
   a. Read them together with the class.
   b. Reread them slowly. Point to each word as you read.
   c. Ask students to raise their fingers when you see the verb.

3. The next two sentences (c and d)
   a. Read them together with the class.
   b. Ask students to turn to their neighbor to share the verb or action word.
   c. Ask them to tell their neighbor how they know it's a verb.

4. Last two sentences (e and f)
   a. Students having thinking (scratch) paper
   b. Read sentences together with the class.
   c. Ask students to write the verb on their thinking paper.
   d. Quickly circulate to see who's got it.
   e. Repeat with each.

5. Riddle: I'm thinking of a verb.
   a. It's something we'll be doing on today's worksheet (writing).
   b. It's something you do with your hand when you want to be called on (raise).
   c. It's something you do at the fountain.

IV. INDEPENDENT PRACTICE ACTIVITY

1. Students will be given the verb worksheet (see textbox 7.6).
2. May need to read the sentences aloud to some students.

MATERIALS/RESOURCES REQUIRED

Smart Board, computer, worksheets (see next), thinking paper.

Textbox 7.8 Example of a skills lesson plan to teach verbs

Verb Worksheet

Directions: In each sentence that follows, underline the verb or the action word.

1. He was washing the dishes.
2. It is time to go home.
3. Please take out your pencils.
4. She kicked the ball hard.
5. They were eating lunch.
6. Molly slipped on the ice.
7. Pat ran outside.
8. Sally kicked the ball hard.
9. Bill was working hard.
10. Pam was sleeping on the carpet.

Textbox 7.9 Verb worksheet

FINAL WORD

Every teacher, of every subject, at every level, teaches some type of skill. The elements of effective skills instruction will enhance your ability to do this.

Part III

LEARNER-CENTERED INSTRUCTION

Teacher-centered instruction and learner-centered instruction provide two distinctly different ways of thinking about the teaching and learning experience. The difference between these approaches is not in what is taught; rather, how it is taught. The next three chapters focus on instructional models that are *learner-centered*.

CHARACTERISTICS OF LEARNER-CENTERED INSTRUCTION

The characteristics of learner-centered instruction described later are based on the 14 Psychological Principles of Learner-Centered Instruction put forth by the American Psychological Association. (visit their website: https://www. apa.org/ed/governance/bea/learner-centered.pdf) Instructional strategies that are learner-centered contain some or all of the following six characteristics:

1. **Learning experiences are open ended.** Students are not always expected to come to a predetermined conclusion or to create a standardized product. This does not mean that there are no standards or defined bodies of knowledge and skills that they must know and learn. Rather, students are often able to go beyond a predefined answer or to come to their own conclusions based on the data or experience.

2. **Students have choices.** Choice includes things, such as topics to study, ways to learn and demonstrate learning, books to read, topics about which to write, assignment descriptions, and due dates. Choice here does not mean total choice all the time; rather, choice is found on a continuum with four degrees of choice (see figure 3.1). Learner-centered instruction can vary among the four middle choice options depending on students and the situation.

total choice all the time	total choice some times	some choice some times	choice within a set of options	no choice some times	no choice ever

chaos --- structure ------------------------------------- control

Figure Part III 1   Continuum of choices

3. **Knowledge is presented in meaningful contexts.** New knowledge is best learned in the context of preexisting knowledge and personal experiences (National Research Council, 2000). Thus, instruction, assignments, and activities are designed to make connections with what students know or have experienced. Also, learner-centered instruction often includes thematic or integrated curriculums that are used to integrate new knowledge in a variety of contexts. Here, artificial curriculum boundaries become blurred. This enables concepts and skills to be visited numerous times in a variety of settings.

4. **Social interaction is valued.** Social interaction is viewed as a way of engaging students in higher-level thinking and deeper learning (O'Donnell, 2006). In learner-centered instruction, students are asked to share with and to respond to the ideas of others. Cooperative learning, student conversation, and other types of human interaction are considered valuable tools to enhance learning.

5. **Students are actively engaged in the learning process.** Information and ideas are applied, practiced, reinforced, or manipulated during the learning process to the greatest extent possible. It is through active engagement that learners are able to use preexisting knowledge and new information to construct new knowledge (National Research Council, 2000).

6. **Learning experiences are based on the learner's natural desire to learn.** Humans are perceived as whole and complete entities with an innate desire to find out about the world around them (Maslow, 1971; Rogers & Freiberg, 1994). Learning experiences are designed to complement this natural desire to learn, grow, self-actualize and fully develop one's full potential. Real learning is viewed as a pleasurable, intrinsically motivating experience. Learner-centered instruction is predicated on the idea that active exploration and problem solving are natural and more powerful ways to learn (Bruner, 1977). In contrast, learning in which students are manipulated through the use of extrinsic rewards and punishments is seen as unnatural, ineffective, and dehumanizing.

LESS-DIRECT INSTRUCTION

The form of instruction associated with learner-centered instruction is *indirect instruction*. Whereas direct instruction strategies work best for teaching facts, rules, and basic skills, indirect instruction strategies works best for teaching concepts, theories, patterns, and abstractions (Borich, 2006). However, the term "indirect instruction" can be a bit misleading. Some people incorrectly assume that there is no teaching involved here or that this type of instruction does not require thoughtful planning. Not true on both accounts. To avoid this confusion, the term *"less direct instruction"* (LDI) is used here.

Comparing Direct and Less-Direct Instruction

Analyze the two lessons plans given next. Both lessons teach the same objectives. As you compare these two types of lessons, what do you notice? How are they the same? How are they different? Which lesson would you prefer to teach? Which lesson do you think would result in greater learning? Why?

#1 Direct Instruction—Teacher-Centered Grade 2/3

Purpose Statement: Students will learn about applying science skills: measuring, weighing, observing counting, and recording.

Behavioral Objective: Students will demonstrate their learning by measuring, weight, observing/counting, and record important potato data.

Materials: potatoes, rulers, scales, data charts (DCs)

Input:

1. Scientists study the world we live in.
   a. need skills to describe and compare things

2. Scientists study the world by collecting data.
   a. data are information
   b. get data by measuring, observing, recording, and counting

3. Science describes things using data
   a. describe our class by collecting data
   b. number of students, girls, boys
   c. describe classroom, length

4. Others describe things using based on what they think/feel.
   a. not science
   b. feeling—classroom seems fun, exciting, colorful

5. Examples
   a. science—the dog is three years old, has black fur, weighs twenty-seven pounds.

b. not-science—the dog is cute, it is excited, it knows lots of tricks, looks like my dog Fluffy.

Guided Practice/Activity

1. Hand out potatoes and DC (see next).
2. Have students measure length and width of potato, and record data on DC.
3. Have students weigh a potato and record data on DR.
4. Have students count the number of eyes and record on DR.
5. Have students observe a potato, draw a picture on DC, and record interesting or important traits, characteristics (color, texture, etc.)
6. Make a potato graph (graphing one statistic such as weight, length, weight, width, # of eyes).

Extension

7. Make a different graph each day for different potato statistics.
8. Do the same with a carrot, a gerbil, a rock, and a person.

Integrated potato studies: Potato art, potato books, create a potato drama, describe the potato (language arts), potato math problems, science/social studies (how potatoes are grown), potato science experiments (potatoes in water; observe/record what happens; compare one in light one in darkness)

Teacher: Consult the curriculum to decide on future lessons.

Textbox Part III 1

#2 Less Direct Instruction—Learner Centered—Grade 2/3

Purpose Statement: Students will learn about applying science skills: measuring, weighing, observing counting, and recording.
Behavioral Objective: Students will demonstrate their learning by measuring, weight, observing/counting, and recording important potato data.
Materials: potatoes, rulers, scales, DCs

Input/Activity

1. Give students potatoes, rulers, scales, and lots of time for them to mess around for a bit.
2. Ask students to describe their potatoes.

3. Ask who's is the biggest? Heaviest? How do you know? How can we describe our potatoes so that another class will know exactly what our potatoes look like? How can we quickly compare our potatoes? What data might be important to record?

4. Task: You are scientists. Important skills for scientists are to weigh measure, count, observe, and record. You are studying potatoes. We need to get your potato data so we can compare potatoes for our potato study. (Give students the DC.) These are the data we need from you: length, wide, weight, # of eyes.

5. How can we show the weight of all our potatoes quickly? If somebody wanted to know how much all our potatoes weighed quickly, how could we do this? What do we use to quickly show numeral data? (bar graph)

6. Put students into groups by statistical data: weight, length, width, and # of eyes. Give each group a DC for creating graphs to keep track of getting individual data. Let each group create their own bar graphs.

Extension

7. Make a different graph each day for different potato statistics.
8. Do the same with a carrot, a gerbil, a rock, and a person.

Integrated potato studies: Potato art, potato books, create a potato drama, describe the potato (language arts), potato math problems, science/social studies (how potatoes are grown), potato science experiments (potatoes in water; observe/record what happens; compare one in light one in darkness)

Teacher: Observe students' interests and deficiencies and consult curriculum for future lessons.

Textbox Part III 2

In the lesson plan examples discussed in the previous section, notice where the activity or experience is in relation to instruction. Whereas direct instruction provides instruction up front and an activity or experience to reinforce the instruction, less-direct instruction is often based on or in the experience. Students generally have some sort of experience first so that they are able to put the instruction that follows in some sort of meaningful context. Described in this section are three forms of less-direct instruction: discovery learning, problem-based learning, and inquiry.

Chapter 8

Discovery Learning

This chapter describes *discovery learning*. Like direct instruction, discovery learning is not a method or an approach to teaching; it is a pedagogical strategy (one of many), which can be used to enhance learning. Discovery learning first exposes students to some sort of structured experience in order for them to discover some of the defining attributes, concepts, or principles inductively (Johnson, 2009). Explicit instruction is then provided along the way as necessary.

Discovery learning is sometimes mischaracterized as unstructured chaos, without defined objectives, planning, or assessment. However, as you will see further, this is not the case. Discovery learning is a pedagogical strategy that comes in a variety of forms with varying degrees of structure, all of which require careful planning. Remember, no single strategy works best for all students all the time. Like any of the strategies described in this book, discovery learning should be used at specific times for specific purposes.

OPEN AND GUIDED DISCOVERY

Two categories of discovery learning are presented here: open discovery learning and guided discovery learning.

Open Discovery Learning

Open discovery learning (ODL) is seldom used in its purest form. This is on the far end of the discovery learning continuum as it utilizes the least amount structure. Here students make all decisions related to all aspects of learning and they come to their own conclusion based on data or experience with no input or guidance from the teacher. There are few situations where this level of unstructured, open-discovery learning would be effective (students need structure in varying degrees and form).

• **The research paper.** The process used to write a research paper is a common form of ODL. It is open ended and involves a fair amount of choice on the part of the learner; however, structure is necessary for students to be successful. Next you will see steps that can be used with students at the middle or high school level. These steps provide structure to guide learners in this type of ODL. This structure can be simplified for use with elementary and intermediate students.

Steps for writing a research paper

1. Choose a topic.
2. Put your topic in the form of one to three questions. These questions will guide you in the collection of your data (notes).
3. Identify potential sources (books, articles, interviews, Internet sites, surveys, etc.)
4. Read critically and take notes (data).
5. Examine your notes looking for groups or patterns and create an initial outline for your research paper (inductive analysis).
6. Create an initial draft. Get feedback. Reread and revise often.
7. Complete the editing process.

Textbox 8.1

• **Independent study or investigation.** An independent study or investigation is also a form of discovery learning. These can be conducted individually, in pairs, or in a small group. Here, learners ask a question then gather data to answer the question. After answering their question, learners present their findings using some type of form (lab report, presentation, video, poster, or other). The steps that follow show the structure necessary to design this type of learning experience. The type and amount of structure you use here will be dependent on the learners and situations. Independent studies can be modified to fit students at all ages, grades, and ability levels.

Steps for an independent study

1. The learner identifies a topic and puts it in the form of a question.
2. The learner fills out a Plan to Investigate form (figure 8.1).
3. The learner meets with the teacher to get an approval for the independent study.

4. The teacher and learner agree upon a method to collect and organize data.
5. The teacher and learner agree upon a time frame in which to complete the independent study and present the results.
6. The learner collects and organizes data.
7. The learner makes a conclusion or develops findings based on the data.
8. The learners present data and conclusions/findings to the class or in some other forum.

Textbox 8.2

An independent study or investigation of any kind is highly dependent on first identifying an appropriate question or questions. At this stage, you can help students identify a question based on the curricular goals.

Knowing the criteria used to assess a project before beginning reduces stress and enables them to focus on the specific elements. The given criteria can be simplified for elementary students.

Criteria for an independent study

_____ 1. Meets deadlines.
_____ 2. Obtains necessary background knowledge.
_____ 3. Uses appropriate methods to gather data.
_____ 4. Gathers an appropriate amount of data.
_____ 5. Comes to appropriate conclusions based on the data.
_____ 6. Prepares and makes a presentation to share data and findings.

Textbox 8.3

Key: 3 = above criteria; 2 = criteria met; 1 = criteria partially met; 0 = criteria not met

Students should complete the plan to investigate form (see figure 8.1) prior to beginning the project. It provides ideas for collecting data and enables the teacher to approve and provide feedback on the project before beginning. Again, this should be simplified for use with elementary students.

• **Inquiry.** Inquiry is a form of ODL and is described in chapter 10 as a separate strategy.

Guided Discovery Learning

Guided discovery learning (GDL) enables students to construct their understanding of a concept or skill with the guidance of a teacher. This guidance

---

Plan to Investigate

Investigator: _____   Date: _____

....

(before the investigation)
1. What is your topic or special interest?

2. Put your topic or special interest in the form of one or two questions.

3. Important background knowledge (use the back side): Describe three to five important
   things to know about your topic, or interest before you begin.

4. How will you collect data? Check one.
       read ___   measure__   interview___   time____   survey___   questionnaire___

       weigh ___   listen___   observe ___   count ___   checklist ___   other ____

5. When will you present your findings to the class? _____

6. How will you present your data and findings? Check one.
       lab report ___   graph_____   poster ___   lab report ___   visual art ___   web site ___

       photos ___   brochure ___   video_____   graphic org. ___   poem___   other ___

Teacher approval to continue: _____Date: _____

(This top section must be completed before continuing)
....

(after the investigation)
7. Organize your data. Look for groups or patterns. Create order. Use tables or graphs to
   organize numerical information.

8. What findings or general conclusions can you make based on the data

---

Figure 8.1   Plan to investigate form

comes in the form of questions, hints, modeling, and short bits of instruction. Learning here contains elements of open-endedness in which students
often discover things beyond the lesson purpose or objective. However, it is
also explicit and defined in that there are specific skills or concepts that the
teacher wants students to possess as a result of the learning experience. With
GDL, the teacher acts as a coach to correct misinformation, to supply necessary missing information, and to make sure students get to the right conceptual place. Examples of guided discovery are described further.

• **Discovering a concept.** In teaching concepts using guided discovery,
students are asked to use inductive reasoning to determine the principles or
defining attributes of a concept. The basic steps are presented here.

Steps for discovering a concept:

1. Provide students with several examples of the concept. Ask them if they can perceive any similarities or common attributes.
2. Provide nonexamples and ask students to compare with examples in order to note differences.
3. Ask students to identify the defining attributes of the concept.
4. Presents the name and definition of the concept.
5. Makes corrections or additions to students' list of defining attributes.
6. As a form of guided practice, ask students to identify other examples and nonexamples of the concept. They should be able to summarize principles or main concepts at this point.
7. Create a concept map or graphic organizer at the end of the lesson to describe the concept and the ordinate, superordinate, and subordinate relationships within that concept.

Textbox 8.4

For example, Mr. Harris is teaching the concept of a triangle to his 1st grade students. He shows them several examples of different types of triangles on a large poster. Students are asked to identify what is the same about all the shapes. He guides students when necessary. *"What kind of lines to you see? Are they straight or are they crooked?"* Mr. Harris lists the following attributes on a poster: three pointed corners, three straight sides, and a closed shape. He tells students that these are all shapes called triangles and he reviews the attributes. Mr. Harris then presents a variety of shapes that are not triangles. He tells his students they are not triangles (squares, circles, lines, open shapes, etc.). He compares the nonexample to the attribute. "This shape has four sides. It can't be a triangle. This shape has a curvy line. It can't be a triangle." Students are then presented with a set of flat, wooden blocks cut in a variety of shapes. They are asked to find and create a group that only has triangles in it.

Table 8.1 shows the difference between GDL and expository teaching for concept teaching. So which form of teaching should you use? Both. No single pedagogical strategy should be used exclusively. Different students respond differently to different strategies at different times.

• **Events, examples, or experiences (3-E).** A planned series of events, examples, or experiences can also be used for discovery learning. For example, a teacher might plan several related field trips. Students would be asked to

Table 8.1   Comparing expository teaching and discovery learning

TEACHING A CONCEPT

Discovery Learning—Jerome Bruner	*Expository Teaching—David Ausubel*
* *Provide examples, then use inductive reasoning to determine the principle*	* *Explain the principles, then use deductive reasoning to determine if examples are in alignment with the principles.*
1. Provide examples and nonexamples 2. Students identify common attributes 3. Describe defining attributes 4. Name and define the concept 5. Present concept map	1. Present advanced organizer (concept map) 2. Name and define the concept 3. Describe relevant and irrelevant attributes 4. Provide examples and nonexamples 5. Students identify examples and nonexamples

note common elements after each trip. A teacher could also plan and present a series of video scenarios, dramas, models, music, books, stories, web sites, or other educational events, examples, or experiences. Between each, students would be asked to identify common elements. This list should be flexible and continually changing until the last example or event.

For example, Ms. Lewis is teaching various literary genres in her 4th-grade literacy class. She wants her students to understand the concept of historical fiction. Over the course of a week, she has her students read several short historical fiction excerpts. Each day, students are asked to describe interesting or important things related to the story and the specific attributes (e.g., past time period, characters that did not exist). She uses questions to guide them here if they seem to have trouble. She then asks them what the author used to make the story interesting to read. Each day, students' ideas are recorded or displayed on butcher paper. At the end of the week, she describes the particular genre category and its attributes. Students compare this with the attributes for fiction and historical books. Students are then asked, "What makes a good historical fiction book?" After a discussion in which students' ideas are recorded on the board, each student lists four to six attributes in his or her reading log. Students are then allowed a choice of historical fiction chapter books to read. After each chapter, students record interesting or important ideas in the reading log and rate the chapter on the attributes described.

• **Flipping.** Flipping is a form of GDL where the established order of things is reversed or flipped. Here students first have exposure to the new material through reading or lecture videos. In high school and higher education, this often occurs outside of class. Then, class time is used to assimilate the knowledge learned through strategies like problem solving, discussion, small group speeches (Small group speeches), debate, or activities that would normally be considered homework.

• **Guided discovery for skills instruction.** Here students are first immersed in an experience or an activity in which they need one or more skills. Individual skills are taught as students are ready for them or as they discover a need. Students should be given plenty of time and materials for experimenting. You will often see teachers asking students, "What have you discovered?" For example, guided discovery for skills instruction can occur in science class where students are given a problem to solve and the necessary materials with the objective of learning specific skills related to scientific inquiry (weighing, measuring, observing, inductive analysis, recording, etc.). As one or more student discovers the correct uses of one of these skills, the teacher calls the entire class's attention to it and does a short mini-lesson.

One note of caution: While exploration is a powerful element in learning, you want to avoid too much fishing around. Freedom taken too far can result in chaos or frustration. Instead, try to find the zone of proximal development just above the independent level and below the frustration level to introduce and formally teach the desired skill.

For example, Mr. Green is teaching interpersonal communication skills in this 9th grade humanities class. He leads students through a series of small group activities designed to highlight specific interpersonal skills. After each activity, he asks students, "What did you notice about [insert skill]?" He then asks, "What would be a good rule for that we could add to our list of communication skills?" As students list ideas, he guides them in the description of specified interpersonal skills. In using this strategy, students often describe skills for which he had not planned. These are also included in the list. After each small-group activity, one or two skills are added to the list of important communication skills.

DISCOVERY LEARNING LESSON PLAN

This lesson plan format in textbox 8.1 was introduced in chapter 1. It provides an apt overview of discovery learning.

I. Purpose Statement:

1. The concept, topic, or skill you want students to learn.
2. Example: Students will learn about/how to [*insert concept, topic, or skill here*].

II. Discovery Activity:

1. Identify elements you want students to discover.

2. Design discovery activity that enables discovery of some or all of these elements.
3. After the discovery activity, students are asked to identify or describe salient elements.

III. Input:

1. Students are provided specific information related to lesson purpose
2. Input is used to fill in the blanks or extend initial discoveries

IV. Activity/Independent Practice:

1. Used to reinforce, extend, practice, or apply their learning
2. Use or apply the concept, topic, or skill in some fashion

Textbox 8.5 Discovery learning lesson plan

FINAL WORD

Discovery learning can be a powerful learning strategy; however, to be effective, it must be purposeful and planned. As well, discovery learning is one strategy. No single strategy should be used exclusively.

Chapter 9

Problem-Based Learning

Students' problem-solving skills can be developed by directly teaching them effective problem-solving strategies and then providing them with opportunities to practice these strategies (Johnson, 2009). The ideas and strategies described in this chapter can be taught to students to enhance their problem-solving abilities in a variety of contexts.

PROBLEMS

A *problem* can be defined as a situation in which the present condition, product, or performance does not match the desired condition, product, or performance. Problem solving is the process of moving from the present to the desired condition, product, or performance.

The Power of Real Problems

Students should, whenever possible, be engaged in *real problems*. Sometimes referred to as an *ill-structured problem,* real problems reflect real-world events (Sternberg & Williams, 2010). Real problems are real, not riddles to be solved or mathematical word problems with one correct answer found in the teacher's manual. Real problems are also those for which the teacher does not have an answer. And the nice thing about real problems is that the real world is filled with them. Using these real-world problems serves to create a bridge between the curriculum and the world in which students live.

TWO PROBLEM-SOLVING STRATEGIES

Two very useful and pragmatic problem-solving strategies are *creative problem solving* and *means end analysis*. There are many more complicated models; however, these strategies are simple and can be used at all grades and levels.

Creative Problem Solving

In using *Creative Problem Solving* (CPS) you first define the problem and then generate as many ideas as possible for solutions. The key to successful implementation of this strategy is to produce a large number of ideas. Thus, there should be no evaluation of your initial ideas as this would prevent the full range of possibilities from being explored. It is only after all possible ideas are generated and listed that you should engage in any sort of evaluative discussion. This is where you look to choose one idea that seems to be the best. And often, two or three of the ideas will be combined for the solution. This would not be possible had you not first generated many ideas. The final steps are to refine, implement, and evaluate the solution. The steps for CPS are listed in textbox 9.1.

CPS

1. Define the problem.
2. Generate as many solutions as possible.
3. Choose a solution that seems the best.
4. Elaborate and refine.

Textbox 9.1 Thinking Frame for CPS

The graphic organizer in figure 9.1 can be used to guide students thinking in the CPS process. Working alone, with a partner, or in groups, students first define the problem, then generate and list their ideas in the column on the left.

Means End Analysis

In using *Means End Analysis* (MEA), you begin by describing the desired state. "What is the goal?" "What outcome would I like to occur?" "What would it look like if this problem were solved?" Next, analyze and describe the current state. Then, generate a list of steps or conditions necessary to get to the desired state. These steps or conditions can be in random order here. Finally, construct a plan that will move you from point A (current state) to point B (desired state). The steps for this final plan should be listed in chronological order. The steps for MEA are listed in textbox 9.2.

Problem:	
Ideas:	Initial solution/plan: Elaborate and refine:

Figure 9.1   CPS graphic organizer

MEA

1. Describe the desired state.
2. Describe the current state.
3. Generate a list of necessary steps or conditions.
4. Construction and implement a plan.

Textbox 9.2 Thinking frame for MEA

The graphic organizer in figure 9.2 can be used to guide students' thinking processes. Just like the CPS graphic organizer discussed previously, students can work individually, with a partner, or in groups in using this.

PROBLEM-BASED LEARNING

Problem-based learning is simply embedding problems into the curriculum to enhance learning and problem solving (Johnson, 2009). This section describes ideas for this process

Embedding Problem Solving in a Lesson or Unit

Once you have taught students the problem-solving process, you can begin looking for ways to embed problems into lessons or units. Keep in mind that problem solving is being described here as a teaching strategy to enhance or extend learning. That is, it is a way for students to manipulate content at deeper levels. Problem-solving activities can range in complexity from simple classroom activities that are of short duration and do not require additional resources, to the more complex independent projects that require students to get background information, create supplemental materials, and design a formal presentation.

Goal/End State:
Current State:
Necessary Steps/Things to Do:
The Plan:

Figure 9.2   MEA graphic organizer

Personal and Interpersonal Problem Solving

Problem solving can also be used to address personal and interpersonal problems. A small group provides a safe environment for students to explore options and alternatives for the problems they may face or be experiencing or will face. It also provides students with a variety of ideas and perspectives. Further discussed are four ideas for using problem solving for these types of issues:

First, find interpersonal problems or personal decisions from a story the class is reading, or from history and current events. If possible, look for problems that might be related to a problem or decision that your students might encounter.

Second, choose a common problem that students at your grade level seem to face. For younger children, this might be something like encountering a bully or teasing on the playground. For older students, it might be something like dealing with peer pressure or an unfair situation involving a teacher or parent.

Third, for a journal prompt or writing activity, ask students to identify and describe a problem from their life. Next, have students move into small groups to share what they have written. Then, ask students to try select one of the problems and use one of the problem-solving strategies. Finally, students would individually describe the problem and the solution they would use. This becomes a powerful writing activity because they are engaged in authentic writing related to real-life issues. However, a great amount of caution and discretion should be used here. This is not an activity to do the first month of a school year. You need to know your students before you move into these types of activities. You also need make sure that trust and respect have been established. Finally, encourage students to write only about those things they feel comfortable in sharing in a small group. Let them know that there are other times and places to talk about deeply personal issues.

And fourth, select problems found in Dear Abby or some other advice columns to use for problem-solving activities. Small groups can compare their answer with the advice the columnist gave at the end of the activity. Again, discretion and a thorough knowledge of your students should be used in selecting the types of problems to be examined here. It can be made into an authentic writing activity by asking students to describe the problem and their solution.

FINAL WORD

Problem-based learning is simply a matter of insert problems into a curriculum, or building a lesson or curriculum around problems. Two simple problem-solving strategies were described here: CPS and MEA.

Chapter 10

Inquiry Learning

METHODS OF SCIENCE

Inquiry learning uses methods of science as a pedagogical strategy to enhance learning (Johnson, 2009). There are a variety of scientific methods. This chapter describes three methods: (a) creating groups or inductive analysis, (b) surveys and interviews, and (c) inquiry experiments. These are all examples of the types of inquiries used by real scientists to examine the world. With each of these methods, a question is first asked, and then data are used to answer that question.

Creating Groups: Inductive Analysis

Creating groups is a scientific methodology in which the researcher observes a field in order to understand it. Here, data are collected through observation. As the data are collected and recorded, the researcher uses inductive analysis to organize them into groups or categories. Finally, the researcher describes the field in terms of those groups. Here questions are generally asked about the make up of a larger whole (see next). The following are examples of three inquiry activities that use inductive analysis.

Questions used for creating groups inquiry

- What kinds of beverages do students drink at lunch?
- What rocks are found in the parking lot?
- What activities occur at recess?
- What kinds of activities occur in the mezzanine before school?

- What kinds of adjectives are used in this chapter?
- What kinds of stories are found on the front pages of most newspapers?
- What kinds of things do students read in the library?

Textbox 10.1

Examples of Inquiry Projects Using Inductive Analysis

• **Observe behaviors.** To answer a question related to the types of behaviors occurring at a particular place, students would go to a place to examine the various types of behaviors occurring. An initial visit should be made to get a sense of the behaviors that occur there (pilot study). The types of behaviors are used to create categories that are then used for headings for a *data retrieval chart* (DRC) (see figure 10.1). A DRC is any graphic organizer that is used to gather and organize information.

For example, students in Mr. Kerry's 10th grade class conducted an inquiry to answer the question: "What kinds of behaviors occur in the high school study hall?" A small group of students identified the following behaviors during an initial pilot study: talking, sleeping, reading/studying, games, and cell phones or computers. These categories were used as headings on a DRC.

The next day these students observed behaviors and put tally marks in the appropriate category each time one of the behaviors was observed. Then they used this information to create a table that described the type and frequency of the behaviors (see table 10.1). These data were also displayed using graph (see figure 10.2). Next, students used this information to make comparisons over time as well as to compare study hall behaviors at various times during the day. To extend this, they compared the behaviors of males and females and older and younger students.

Study Hall Behavior

Behavior➜	Talking	Sleeping	Reading/Studying	Games	Cell Phone Computer

Figure 10.1   DRC for study hall inquiry project

Table 10.1   Table showing study hall behaviors

Behavior	Number
Talking	29
Reading/studying	15
Cell phones/computer	14
Games	4
Sleeping	2

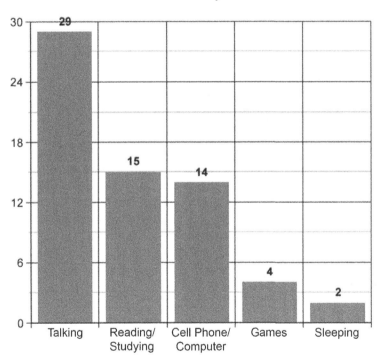

Figure 10.2   Graph showing study hall behaviors

• **Story events.** The question was: "What interesting or important things happened in this story?" After reading a chapter of the book, the students in Ms. Lynch's 5th grade reading class brainstormed and created a list of twenty-seven important or memorable events. Then, they used inductive analysis to find groups within the list. Next, they moved items into groups and recorded the number of events in each group. Finally, the students described the results in terms of groups and numbers within each group. Like discussed earlier, the data were displayed in both graph and table form. To extend this activity, Ms. Lynch asked students to use the same groups to compare chapters, books, and authors.

• **Observation of current events.** The question was: "What interesting or important events occurred during the week?" At the end of the week, the students in Mr. Carter's 7th grade class worked in small groups to examine newspapers and record the events that were printed on the front page that week. These events were analyzed and put in groups. The events were then described in terms of groups and numbers within each group. After a few weeks, students began to notice patterns. After five weeks, students created graphs to show change in the number and kinds of events occurring over time. This activity was extended by having students use their categories to examine events reported in newspapers during the last year.

Surveys and Interviews

This second type of inquiry is dependent on first identifying a research question or area of interest. Students then design some type of survey or interview to collect data that will answer the research question. Surveys and interviews can be used to access information from students' family, friends, or people in the community. Also, current online technology can be used with both to expand students' access to a wider audience. There are a variety of free online survey programs that can be adopted and adapted for use. As well, email, Skype, discussion groups, chat groups, and other communication programs can be used for interviews or surveys.

Surveys. Survey activities can be designed for students as early as the primary grades. These surveys should have only one or two questions or use logos or pictures to guide responses. For example, Mr. Pritzker asked his kindergarten students to identify their favorite desert. A large chart was set up that had pictures of four different desert choices. Students put an x on the chart to identify their favorite desert. Survey data can be collected using two different types of survey questions: open ended and closed response.

• *Open-ended survey questions.* An open-ended question is one that allows respondents unlimited choices. For example, if the inquiry question was, "What kinds of music do students in our grade like to listen to?" An open-ended question to use here would be either, "What kinds of songs do you like to listen to? Or "What are some of your favorite songs?" Some respondents may provide four or five responses, while others may only report one. The researcher then uses inductive analyses (discussed earlier in the book) to create categories. As discussed earlier, the categories and numbers within each category can be reported using graphs or tables. Open-ended questions provide a more accurate sense of what respondents are thinking when compared to closed-response questions; however, these types of survey questions are somewhat messy in terms of analysis.

• *Closed-response questions.* A closed-response question provides a number of choices for respondents to select. For example, to answer the same inquiry question discussed earlier, the survey question could be: *What is your favorite music genre: (a) country, (b) pop/contemporary, (c) hip-hop or rap, (d) vocal/choral, (e) classical/instrumental, or (d) other* ___. This type of question enables students to include several questions in the survey and get quantifiable data on many types of issues quickly. For example, after surveying a group of people with the question discussed earlier, students could safely report that 84.4 percent of respondents surveyed preferred country as a musical genre. The problem with these kinds of questions is that they can be inaccurate, misleading, or controlling. For example, what if the first music choice of a respondent was not listed on the question discussed earlier? Or what if a respondent liked to listen to three or four different kinds of music equally well?

With a little imagination, inquiries using surveys can be designed to enhance learning in any curricular area. Some examples of the types of questions that might be asked are listed in figure 10.5. Also, the Internet has surveys and polls on a wide variety of topics that have already been conducted and which can be incorporated into all curriculum areas to add depth and dimension to lesson content. To find these, use the Internet search terms: "survey" or "poll" along with the topic of study for which you are looking.

Examples of possible survey inquiry questions

• What is your favorite beverage?
• How do you think the book should have ended?
• What sport or game do most students enjoy playing?
• Who do students admire?
• What kinds of TV shows are most popular?
• What are students' favorite book or books?
• How do students use the Internet?
• What do students think is the most important event that happened this year?
• What kinds of problems do students have in their lives?
• What kinds of books do students in our class enjoy reading?
• What traits do students look for in a friend?
• What method do you use to ask somebody for a date?

Textbox 10.2   Examples of questions for inquiry surveys

Interviewing. Interviews enable students to get information directly from others and can be adapted for use with students as early as 1st grade. Here the researcher prepares a set of questions in advance of the interview. What is given up in terms of quantity of questions is gained in the depth of responses. While surveys enable researchers to get basic information from many people; interviews allow researchers to get in-depth information from a few. Also, the interview format allows the researcher to ask follow-up questions, to seek clarification, and to ask the interviewee to expand on interesting or important information that comes up during the interview.

Four tips for using interviews: First, students at all grade levels need help preparing interview questions initially. With younger students, it is recommended that most, if not all interview questions be prepared for them initially. They will eventually learn how to ask their own questions. Second, an interview should contain four to ten open-ended questions with possible follow-ups for each question. For primary age students, interviews should contain one to four questions. A common mistake beginning interviewers at all levels make is to have too many questions. Third, students should spend time practicing and conducting interviews in class with classmates before conducting interviews outside the classroom. Conducting these types of interviews is also an effective way to practice communication skills and to address interpersonal, social, and emotional elements. And fourth, have students use an audio tape to record the interview (if possible) and then go back and take notes after the interview is completed.

Examples of Inquiry Projects Using Surveys and Interviews

• **Open-ended survey activities.** Ms. Lew's 7th grade class was studying media as part of their social studies curriculum. Ms. Lew posed the question to her students, "What kinds of music do you thinking students at Frederic Middle School like to listen to?" After a couple of hypotheses, she asked, "As social scientists, how do you think we can get this information?" She then helped her students set up an inquiry activity using open-ended surveys. After coordinating with the rest of the teachers in the building, small groups of social scientists were sent to different classrooms with clip boards. They identified asked students in each classroom, "What music do you like to listen to?" They could list up to three songs for each student surveyed.

After three days, every classroom in the school had been surveyed. After an initial look at the answers on their clips boards, students settled on the following categories: (a) country, (b) pop-rock, (c) rap and hip-hop, (d) hard rock, (e) vocal/choral, (f) soul, and (g) other. Each student then put the music genres into groups and tallied up the numbers in each group. After the totals were collected, the class then described the music listening preferences of the students at Frederic Middle School in terms of categories and numbers within each category. As part of their language arts class, students were then asked to put this information in a graph or table form, and write a lab report (see next). This lab report described the question, how the data were collected, the results, and what the results might mean.

Ms. Lew extended this activity by asking students if they might go about finding the gender differences in students' music listening preferences. Using the seven categories already established, students created a simple DRC where students' responses were recorded with a tally mark (see figure 10.3). If students wanted to compare their school with another school, they could then talk about sample sizes and using percentages versus actual numbers to make comparisons.

• **Closed-response survey activities.** Ms. Perez asked her 4th grade students the following question, "Which sports do students enjoy playing or doing?" And "Do girls like different sports than boys?" A DRC was created using the categories in figure 10.4. Students asked individuals to name their

	Country	Pop Rock	Rap and Hip-Hop	Hard Rock	Vocal, Choral	Soul	Other
Females							
Males							

Figure 10.3   DRC for TV preference project

Sport	Girls	Boys	Total
Swimming			
baseball, softball			
football			
skating			
hockey			
tennis			
track, running			
gymnastics			
volleyball			
wrestling			

Figure 10.4   DRC for favorite sports

favorite sport. Tally marks were used to record the number of responses in each category. These data were quantified and communicated using a table or graph and lab reports were written.

Mr. Duncan asked his 1st grade class, "What lunch do our students like best: pizza, chicken nuggets, hotdogs, or hamburgers?" He created the DRC in figure 10.5 on a piece of poster board. Each student came up and made a tally mark under his or her favorite lunch. The totals were counted and put under each column. In math class, the students used graph paper to create a bar graph showing their results (see figure 10.6). In language arts, the class used the language-experience approach to help students write a simple lab report describing their findings.

• **Interviews.** Ms. Castro's 2nd grade class was studying friendship. The inquiry question was: "What makes a good friend?" Student interviews were set up with students from a 6th grade class. Ms. Castro helped the class brainstorm to create twelve questions. From these, students could select four that they would use for their interview. Each 2nd grade students

Pizza	Chicken Nuggets	Hotdogs	Hamburgers

Figure 10.5   DRC for lunch survey

10				
9	X			
8	X			
7	X			
6	X	X		
5	X	X		
4	X	X		
3	X	X	X	
2	X	X	X	
1	X	X	X	X
	pizza	Chicken nuggets	hotdogs	hamburgers

Figure 10.6   Graph for lunch survey

were paired with a 6th grade student and class time was designated to conduct the interviews. After, Ms. Castro gave the students a lab report template (see below) to provide a scaffold that enabled them to write up their responses. Students then met in small groups of five to share their interviews and results. In the days that followed, Ms. Castro then integrated her friendship unit with students' interviews. In this way, this project was also an example of a GDL.

Students in Mr. Vilsack's 12th grade English class had to interview two people who were age seventy or above. The question was: "What advice can we get from our elders?" Students first submitted proposals priors to their interviews. Here Mr. Vilsack worked with students to help them plan their interviews and design their interview questions. Students then conducted their interviews, gathered and analyzed their data, and wrote up their results in a lab report. Finally, students created visual displays for a poster session. Students from other classes attended.

Experiments

The third type of inquiry, the experiment, is the type of inquiry that most people associate with the scientific method. Like the survey and interview, the researcher first asks a question then uses some procedure to gather data to answer the question. The experiments you use can be fun or even get silly at times. This is acceptable. Remember, you are teaching the processes of conducting scientific inquiries. Also, with inquiry experiments, students will naturally begin to talk about validity, reliability, and sample size (see next). These activities can become excellent vehicles for teaching these advanced scientific concepts as well as having discussions related to ethics in science.

Examples of Experimental Inquiry Projects

• **Gender characteristics.** The question was: "Do males and females perceive gender differently?" Without telling them the question, Ms. Jewell asked for four volunteers to be research subjects in her 8th grade social studies class (two males and two females). The subjects were asked to step outside the laboratory (classroom). The other students in the laboratory then became the scientists whose task it was to observe and record data. After sharing the inquiry question with the class, Ms. Jewell asked them for their initial thoughts on the issue. She then described the experiment and got some of their predictions. Then, one at a time, subjects were asked to come back into the laboratory. They were asked to think of a known female (famous or not), and to describe that person. As the subject described the female, the scientists recorded the type of characteristic mentioned and the order. For example, hair, height, personality, activities, physical stature, or some other characteristic. Each subject was then asked to do the same with a male. The type of characteristics and the order mentioned were again recorded. This process was repeated with all four subjects.

After all the data were collected, Ms. Jewell repeated the inquiry question: *Do students perceive and emphasize different characteristics in males and females? Do boys and girls emphasize different characteristics in their descriptions? Do you think boys and girls perceive gender differently?* She asked students to review their data. After getting some initial ideas, she asked them why they thought they got the results they did and what the data might mean? She also talked about generalizations based on limited sample sized. This led naturally to discussion on how the experiment could be improved. These are the types of questions that all scientists ask. They also reflect the type of ideas often found in the conclusion and discussion sections of research reports. Finally, students were asked to use technical writing to describe the experiment (results and conclusions).

Later that week, students met in small groups to design their own experiment in order to verify the results or to improve the experiment. Some groups decided they needed more subjects, others decided they could answer the question best using survey or interview data. In small groups, the students conducted their own experiments, surveys, and interviews, collected data, answered their question, and wrote up the results. The important point here is that students were engaging in processes of science used by real life researchers.

• **The eyes.** In Ms. Moniz's 6th grade reading class, she was teaching her students about how the brain and the eyes work during the process of reading. As part of this, she created an inquiry/discovery learning project. The inquiry questions were: "How do our eyes move during the act of reading? Do our eyes move differently when reading aloud versus reading silently?" Here, she had students work in groups of three. In each group, one student was designated as the research subject (mouse). The mouse was asked to leave the room as the laboratory (classroom) was prepared. The remaining students (scientists) were given two similar pieces of writing, each containing approximately 100 words, and written at the 5th grade level. The mice returned to the laboratory and were asked to read the first passage silently and then the second passage aloud. The scientists observed the movement of their eyeballs with each reading. After data were collected and the class shared and discussed their findings, students were asked to write and complete their own lab report. Ms. Moniz created the lab report template in textbox 10.1 to enable them to be successful here.

Lab report template

Lab Report
Conditions: This study was designed to study eye movements during reading. We asked a mouse to read a passage silently. We then asked the mouse to read a similar passage aloud.
Results: (Describe your data here. What did you find?)

Condition 1: Reading silently:
Condition 2: Reading aloud:

Conclusions: (What does it mean?)

Textbox 10.3 Lab report template

Ms. Moniz then continued her lesson. Here she described how the brain creates meaning with print; how the eyes use saccades, fixations, and regressions during this meaning-making process; and the implications for studying and comprehending text. Having first done the inquiry project, the information provided in her was much more salient than had she done the lesson without it.

The next day, Ms. Moniz asked students how the experiment might be improved or changed. After getting a variety of ideas, each group was assigned three students from another class to be their laboratory mice. They then conducted their experiment and described their results using a similar lab report. This inquiry project demonstrates how processes of science as well as literacy can move beyond the confines of specified curriculum areas. Students can be reading, writing, and collecting data to answer questions across the curriculum.

• **The boat float.** In his 1st grade classroom, Mr. Burwell constructed boats made from tinfoil that were designed in four different shapes. The question was: *What boat shape holds the most pennies?* Before the experiment, he asked students to make a prediction as to which shape might hold the most pennies and why. He created asimple graph with a picture of each boat shape on the bottom of each row. Students were put in groups of three. Each group went to a learning station that had four tinfoil boats, a pan of water, ten pennies, and a graph. They were asked to see how many pennies they could put in each boat before it sank. To avoid chaos, he designated the following roles: (a) the boater was the person who put the boats in the water and retrieved them, (b) the penny person carefully put the pennies in the boat, and (c) the recorder counted the pennies and filled in the graph. He then guided students through each step of this experiment. After they had tested each boat and filled in their graph, they gathered back in a large group to share and compare their findings. Then, the class decided what they should say for their conclusions. Mr. Burwell recorded their ideas on his computer/ Smart Board screen. Students then used choral reading to practice reading until fluency was achieved.

SCAFFOLDS

You cannot expect students at any age or level to be successful with inquiry activities without creating some sort of structure or scaffold. A scaffold provides the support necessary to enable students to ask questions, collect data, answer their questions, and communicate their finding. After they have become familiar with the process, students at all ages and levels will be able to do each of these independently. Initial scaffolding or support is created three ways: First, provide the initial inquiry questions. As students understand and become familiar with the inquiry process, they will naturally begin asking their own questions. Second, when collecting data, support is provided by designing the DRCs for students to use. As you can see in the previous section, DRC's come in a variety of forms, all of which can be used

Lab Report

Conditions

We wanted to find out what kinds of books 4th and 5th grade students like to read. We also thought it would be interesting to see if boys liked different kinds of books than girls. We created a DRC that had six different kinds of books: (a) action/adventure, (b) comedy, (c) science fiction, (e) horror/thriller, (f) real life, or (f) nonfiction. At recess, we asked students what kinds of books were their favorite as they came out of the cafeteria after lunch. We recorded their answers using tally marks.

Genre	male	female	total
action/adventure			
comedy			
science fiction/fantasy			
horror/thriller			
real life			
nonfiction			

Results.

Type of Movie	Total	Males	Females
comedy	42	18	24
nonfiction	36	20	16
real life	16	12	4
horror/thriller	15	4	11
action/adventure	14	9	5
science fiction/fantasy	11	8	3

Ideas or Conclusions

Comedies were the kinds of books that most 4th and 5th grade students liked. Both boys and girls liked this kind of books. Nonfiction was the second favorite. This was favored pretty much the same by both boys and girls. If we were to pick books for our classroom library, it would be good to get a lot of comedy and nonfiction books.

Figure 10.7   Lab report

to help students organize data as they are collected. And third, use lab report templates to provide support for students when communicating the results of their inquiry projects.

The lab report consists of three parts: the conditions (before), the results (after), and ideas or interpretations (see figure 10.7). "Conditions" describes the research question; what went on before the observation, survey, interview, or experiment; and how students gathered information. "Results" contains just the facts or the data that were collected. Here students report exactly what happened or they present the data collected. If students are doing an inquiry that uses numerical information, they should use graphs, charts, or tables to describe results. In "Ideas or Conclusions" students tell what they think the data might mean or describe how the data could be used.

FINAL WORD

Inquiry is simply asking a question and then collecting and using data to answer questions. It can be used across the curriculum with students as young as kindergarten up through graduate school. There are three basic types of inquiry: creating groups, surveys and interviews, and experiments. With each structure and scaffolding needs to be used until students are able to do inquiry projects independently. Asking the initial question, DRCs and lab reports are all ways to provide structure.

Part IV

USING HUMAN INTERACTION TO ENHANCE AND EXTEND LEARNING

The Importance Of Human Interaction

The chapters in this section describe four strategies that use human interaction in some form to enhance and extend learning: (a) cooperative learning, (b) small group speeches, and (c) class discussions. These can be adopted and adapted for use in all subject areas, and at all ages and levels.

There are seven reasons why you should consider using human interaction as a pedagogical strategy:

1. Human interaction invites students to manipulate ideas at deeper levels as they seek to communicate and understand each other.

2. Human interaction exposes students to a variety of thoughts, perspectives, and thinking styles of which they might not ordinarily be exposed.

3. Interacting with others and working in groups increases student motivation for learning.

4. Human interaction of any kind increases human understanding.

5. Human interaction strategies provide excellent opportunities to teach and practice important interpersonal skills.

6. Human interaction lessens the sense of isolation that some students feel. Social isolation is linked with many problems and disorders, which may include drinking and drugs, depression, and forms of delinquency (Santrock, 2010).

7. Using pedagogical strategies that involve human interaction will teach your students how to function in a group and thus help them get ready to meet the challenges of interacting in a diverse society. If human interaction can do this, it seems silly not to try some of these strategies.

Chapter 11

Cooperative Learning

COOPERATIVE LEARNING IS NOT GROUP WORK

Cooperative learning is a structured teaching and learning strategy in which small teams of students work together using a variety of learning activities to accomplish a shared goal. As you will see in this chapter, it is much different from simply working in a group. It consists of the following five elements:

1. **A specific task**. Cooperative learning starts by identifying a lesson-related learning task for students to accomplish in small groups. This task must be specific. Students should be able to answer yes or no when asked if they have completed the task. Here are examples of nonspecific and specific tasks for cooperative learning groups:

- *Nonspecific task*. As a postreading activity, Ms. Davis asks the groups to discuss chapter 5 in the science text.
- *Specific task*. As a postreading activity, Ms. Davis asks groups to list five interesting or important ideas from chapter 5.
- *Very specific task*. As a postreading activity, Ms. Davis asks each student to list two interesting ideas from chapter 5 individually. Then she has them move into cooperative learning groups of three. Each group will then rank all their ideas from most important to least important. A poster will be created to share with the class.

2. **Positive interdependence**. In a cooperative learning activity, all students must be actively engaged in the completion of the task. They must perceive they cannot succeed unless everyone does his or her part. This element is best achieved by designing activities in which each student has a specific

role or task within the group. Various roles that can be used here are listed as follows:

Roles for Cooperative Learning Activities

1. President: Makes final decisions. Appoints other roles.
2. Reader: Reads the material out loud.
3. Recorder/Scribe: Records ideas.
4. Sociologist: Checks to see how the group is doing on social skills (use matrix).
5. Checker: Checks to make sure everyone's voice or ideas are heard. Makes sure each person has contributed an idea. Sometimes uses a tally mark checklist to indicate who is speaking.
6. Encourager: Looks for good ideas to note and encourages full participation.
7. Speaker/Explainer: Describes the group's decision, explains.
8. Summarizer: Restates the group's major conclusions or answer.
9. Artist: Creates a visual image to correspond with knowing.
10. Dancer/Mime: Creates or performs movement to correspond with assignment.
11. Musician: Sings, performs, describes, or finds songs or song lyrics that correspond with assignment or presentation.
12. Materials Handler: Gets necessary materials to finish the task.
13. Idea Checker: Checks on the learning by asking group members to explain, summarize material.
14. Time Keeper: Keeps track of time.
15. Energizer: Energizes the group when it starts to lag.
16. Webbarian: Gets needed background information or material. Often, this person uses the Internet.
17. Brain: Helps think of answers/ideas.
18. Sound effects: Creates sound effects at appropriate times during a presentation.

Textbox 11.1

In the preceding task, Ms. Davis created positive interdependence by assigning three roles: the president was responsible for making all final decisions and appointing the other roles. Ms. Davis asked the person who last ate vegetables to be the president. This created a chance for social interaction and sharing. A postmaster was responsible for gathering the poster materials and recording the ideas on the poster in order. An artist would be responsible for creating a diagram or picture that would be clued to the poster. When completed, the president found a place in the classroom to hand the poster.

3. **Face-to-face interaction**. When cooperative learning groups are working, students must be seated "knee-to-knee and eye-to-eye" so that they can look at their group mates as they are working together. They should not be working on individual tasks apart from each other. Conversation and interaction are the elements that enable students to grapple with concepts and ideas.

4. **Social skills**. Cooperative learning groups provide a perfect venue to use for teaching social (interpersonal) skills (see figure 11.1). These skills are necessary to function in a group. Before each cooperative learning activity, select one new social skill. Teach it and model or demonstrate what it looks like. Let students know you will be looking for this skill during the cooperative learning activity. During the activity, use anecdotal records or checklists to look for that skill. Figure 11.2 contains an example of a checklist that can be designed for use with a cooperative learning activity. Keep checklists in a three-ring notebook. This will provide a sense of students' performance over time and document the social skills taught. The bottom of the checklist can be used to record general observations and to list social skills to focus on next time. The checklist can also be used to help you recognize and reinforce outstanding use of social skills by individuals or groups at the end of the activity.

5. **Reflection and review**. Allow time at the end of every cooperative learning activity for reflection and review in some form to some degree. This is where groups examine their effectiveness in working together and completing the task. (These two are often related.) The reflection guide in textbox 11.1 can be used to guide this process.

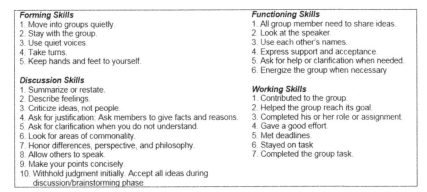

Figure 11.1   Social skills for cooperative learning

Task: _____ *Date:* _____

Key: √ = skill was present; √+ = skill was present to a greater degree;
     √- = skill was present to a lesser degree; # = let's talk.

	Group 1	Group 2	Group 3	Group 4	Group 5
I. FORMING SKILLS					
1. Move quickly and quietly into groups.					
2. Stay with the group.					
3. Use quiet voices.					
4. Take turns.					
II. FUNCTIONING SKILLS					
1. Share ideas and opinions.					
2. Look at the speaker.					
3. Use each other's names.					
4. Express support and acceptance.					
III. DISCUSSION SKILLS					
1. Make your points concisely.					
2. Look for areas of commonality.					
3. Allow others to speak.					
4. Ask for justification.					
IV. WORKING SKILLS					
1. Stayed on task.					
2. Completed individual assignments.					
3. Completed the group task.					

General Notes/Observations:

Figure 11.2   Checklist for social skills

1. Describe things you (the teacher) observed while students were working in cooperative learning groups related to the process.
2. Ask students to describe the things that seemed to go well in their group.
3. Ask students what they would do differently in their group to improve group functioning.
4. Ask students to assess how well their group did in accomplishing its task.

Cooperative Learning Group Reflection

1. Use a checklist similar to that of figure 11.3 to help students focus on specific social skills.
2. Ask groups to give themselves a grade on one or more of the social skills.
3. Ask groups to describe two things the group did well and two things to work on in the next cooperative learning activity.

Individual Reflection

1. Ask students individually to record their observations and ideas in their learning logs.
2. Ask students to assess their own performance on one or more of the social skills.
3. Ask the student to describe the groups' performance in completing the task in their learning log or a short written assignment.

Textbox 11.2 Whole class reflection

TIPS FOR USING COOPERATIVE LEARNING

Cooperative learning is a powerful teaching strategy. Presented here are tips for using cooperative learning.

Tips for Forming Groups

Never ask students to select members for their own groups. This can create undue social pressure on some. Also, student selection tends to create groups that are homogeneous. In most instances, the teacher should select members for cooperative learning groups or some sort of random selection should be used. Teacher-created groups will ensure diversity in terms of gender, ability, age, or other factors such as culture. Random selection to groups can produce some interesting dynamics such as when a student finds himself to be the only male in a group of females.

The following strategies can be used to randomly select members for cooperative learning groups:

• Form groups for students prior to class. One easy way is to enter students' names into a spread sheet or data base in one column and number off in a second column. Then do a sort based on their number. When students enter the room for class, have groups displayed on a screen so they can quickly move into their groups.

• Use a deck of cards. Each student is given a card. Their cooperative learning group would be those who have the same card of another suit.

• Draw for names. Put students' names in a hat and have designated group leaders draw names to determine their group.

• Look for similarities. This method creates random groups of varying sizes. Here you ask students to find classmates who have the same color socks or shirt, a birthday in the same month, or some other factor.

• Form groups based on students' choice. This also creates random groups of varying sizes. Here you write down the names of five to seven different items on the board, such as desert items, board games, fruit, or movies. Students then look at the list and write their favorite on a 3x5 inch card. On the teacher's signal, they then hold up their cards and look for similar choices for their group.

Tips Related to Process

• Take baby steps. It takes time to learn and become comfortable with the design and implementation of cooperative learning activities. Also, students need time to practice and learn this process. Introduce cooperative learning using short, simple tasks. Use groups of two and three students for primary grades and groups of three to five for older students when beginning. If you find that students are having trouble working in cooperative learning groups, make the tasks less complex or the groups smaller.

• Allow a little extra time when planning cooperative learning activities. They generally take more time than other kinds of activities. However, this extra time is offset by the fact that students learn more and learn more deeply.

• Specifying the amount of time students have to complete the task at the outset. Then, as groups are working, provide verbal mile markers by telling students how much time they have left. Also, the use a time keeper as one of the assigned roles helps to keep students on task (see figure 11.1).

• Deemphasis grades. Assigning a grade based on the final product should be used with extreme caution and only on rare occasions. In cooperative learning groups, the process is more important than the product. It is the process of working together that enhances learning. The goal is to enhance learning, not to evaluate or measure students. However, if you insist on evaluating and assigning a grade to a cooperative learning activity, it is strongly recommended that you evaluate your students on the process of working together, and that this be a small part of students' total grade.

THREE COOPERATIVE LEARNING STRATEGIES

The following are examples of three common cooperative learning activities.

There are two types of think-pairs activities:

Think-pair-share. This is a strategy where students are asked a question and given fifteen to thirty seconds to think. It can be helpful to have them list or write down their initial ideas on thinking paper or in a learning log. Then ask students turn to a neighbor to share their ideas. This is a quick and easy way to engage them in learning and for all students' ideas to be heard. It also creates an active learning situation by getting them to interact with the lesson material at a deeper level. You might also say, "Find somebody you have not talked with today." This invites students to interact with a variety of students, some of whom might be outside their normal social groups.

Pairs check. This strategy has students work in pairs to complete an assignment or to solve a problem. One student works to solve the problem or answers a question while the other one observes and checks. The checker can guide or give advice but cannot solve the problem. The conversation that occurs during this process allows students to hear the thoughts of others during the process of problem solving and thus, enhances learning.

Four-Square

Four-Square is a cooperative learning activity that can be adapted for use in a variety of settings. As a postreading activity, students individually record one interesting or important idea from the assigned chapter or book. Next, they bring their idea to their small cooperative learning group. Each group member writes his or her idea in one of the squares on the four-square chart (see figure 11.3). After initial ideas are recorded, students then examine them to see if there is a common element, a big idea, an interesting association, or a conclusion that can be made based on their four initial ideas.

This cooperative learning activity invites students to go beyond the knowledge presented; to synthesize, infer, and look for larger concepts or overriding ideas. Four members seems to work best here; however, sometimes you may have to have a three-square or a five-square group. The following roles can be used here:

- *President:* makes all final decisions and selects people for the other roles,
- *Scribe:* records all ideas on the four-square sheet or poster,

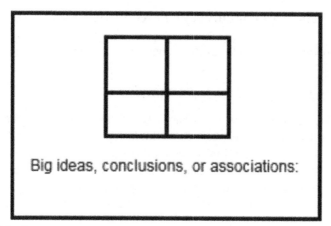

Figure 11.3   Four-square

- *Speaker:* presents ideas and big idea or association to the class, and
- *Artist or mime:* creates a visual picture, design, or nonverbal body movement to illustrate the big idea.

Jigsaw

Jigsaw is a cooperative learning activity in which students begin in a base group. Next, each group member moves to a different expert group where he or she develops specific knowledge in some area. Finally, students return from their expert groups to share their knowledge with their original base group in the creation of some product or performance. It is only by putting all pieces of the puzzle together that the base group is able to accomplish the task.

Example: To help students get ready for a text or an exam, first form base groups. After meeting in their base group, students randomly number off and move into expert groups. Each expert group is given a study guide related to different sections of the upcoming test. The expert group works together to gather information for their section of the test. Finally, students move back into their base groups where each expert shares his or her knowledge with other group members.

FINAL WORD

Cooperative learning is a high-level teaching strategy that takes knowledge, skill, and practice to become fully proficient. Like all pedagogical strategies, cooperative learning is a tool, and like any tool, it can be misused. One misuse of this tool is to use it as only as a measurement device. That is, to grade every cooperative learning activity, or to assign major projects to small groups for which they will receive a grade. Cooperative learning used this way will put undue pressure on some learners. As started earlier, not every activity in a classroom should be evaluated and graded. The purpose of cooperative learning is to enhance learning. As such, the process of working cooperatively in a group is more important than the product. It is the process that enhances learning by enabling your students to manipulate concepts and ideas, to engage in high-level thinking, and to hear a variety of perspectives and thinking styles. The process of working cooperatively also makes learning more enjoyable, increases motivation, and helps students develop important social and interpersonal skills.

Chapter 12

Small Group Speeches

Small group speeches are a strategy that can be used to manipulate lesson input or to examine and explore lesson-related ideas in any subject area at any level. They also provide students who may have difficulties reading and writing another way to demonstrate their learning. Small group speeches are open ended, and hence are an invited choice, challenge, and complexity for any student. Finally, they are a comfortable and effective method to use to teach and practice speaking skills.

THE STEPS

The steps for using small group speeches as a pedagogical tool are as follows:

1. **Identify Elements of Oral Communication (EOC) upon which to focus** (see next). Use direct instruction to define, demonstrate, and teach each of these traits. The EOC are an initial guide for you to use. Once you start observing your students during their speeches, you will have a good sense of what skills needed to be taught. It is recommended that you address two or three elements in a single lesson or activity.

Elements of Oral Communication (EOC)

- Look at your audience.
- Use a moderate pace. Not too fast and not too slow.
- Use inflection. Don't use just a monotone. Make your voice rise and fall to make listening more interesting.
- Controlled stance. Don't lean or slouch.

- Use your hands to emphasis points.
- Pause at important parts.
- Use visual aids.
- Answer questions directly and succinctly.
- Use correct grammar.
- Use known words. Avoid slang or profanity.
- Use words judiciously. Avoid nonwords and nonphrases such as: "um," "well," "you know," and "you guys." Do not use extra words if it can be helped.
- Be concise and to the point. Do not ramble.

Textbox 12.1

2. **Identify a speech topic**. The following are six topic ideas for students' small group speeches:

• *Narrative text, postreading*. Students do a speech as part of a postreading activity. Here they describe two or three interesting or important events or characters from a chapter or story.

• *Textbook postreading*. Students do a speech related to a textbook reading assignment. Here they identify and describe three or four interesting or important ideas from the assigned chapter for their speech. In each group, have different students create speeches from different parts of the text.

• *Postlesson, free choice assignment*. Students do a speech as an alternative to a worksheet or other postlesson assignments. At the beginning of the lesson, alert students to the assignment. Ask them to think about two or three interesting or important ideas for subtopics during the lesson. At the end of the lesson, as students are delivering their speeches, you are able see what and to what degree students have learned.

• *Postlesson, advanced organizer*. Before the lesson, list three to five possible topics on the board as a form of an advanced organizer. Let students know that in their group, each person will be asked to select a different topic for their speech.

• *Unit topics*. Choose a list of speech topics related to the unit you are studying. In small groups, each student selects a different topic for their speech.

• *Some choice*. Students are given a list of unrelated speech topics from which to choose.

• *Free choice*. Students are free to choose any topic for their speech. This type of choice should be used after students have become very familiar with the Small group speeche process.

3. **Create a brainstorming web**. A brainstorming web provides structure as well as content for the speech (see figure 12.1). Teach and demonstrate this

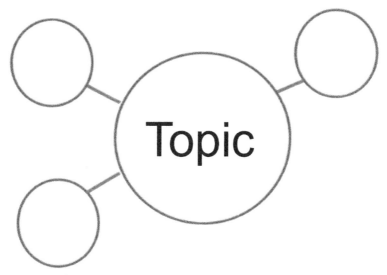

Figure 12.1 **Brainstorming web**

process in large group before asking students to do this individually or in a small group. First, identify a topic and write it inside a circle in the center of a blank piece of paper. Then identify two to three nodes or subtopics and create circles along the outside of the paper for these. Finally, brainstorm to find interesting or important ideas for each subtopic. This brainstorming web is used to guide students' speeches (see next). That is, instead of notes or a written speech, speakers only have the brainstorming web. Therefore, only single words or short phrases should be used to hold ideas.

4. **Deliver the speech**. To speak, students move into groups of three to five. One at a time students stand and deliver their speech to the small group. Another student in the group should be designated as the time keeper and say, "time" when the allotted time is up. These speeches should be no more than one minute in length for middle and high school students and thirty to forty-five seconds for elementary students.

5. **Observe.** During one session, there will be several small group speeches going on at the same time. In this way, you will be able to see and hear many student speeches within a relatively short time.

FEEDBACK

If you want to provide specific feedback related to oral communication, design and use an oral communication checklist similar to that in figure 12.2.

Oral Communication Checklist

Speaker _____   Topic _____

Key: √ = skill was present; √+ = skill was present to a greater degree;
          √- = skill was present to a lesser degree; # = let's talk.

looks at audience	
uses a loud voice	
not too fast or slow (rate)	
controlled stance and hands	

Something done well:

Figure 12.2   Oral communication checklist

You can use this to provide general feedback to the class. Example: *These were the positive things I observed today* . . . You can also use these to document individual students' skills or to provide individual feedback. Here you would select three or four students to observe more specifically during a Small group speeche session. Finally, you can also teach students to use this checklist to give each other feedback.

FINAL WORD

The Small group speeche is a teaching and learning strategy. It is used primarily to extend, apply, reinforce, or manipulate content. It does not take long for students to learn and become comfortable with this process. Small group speeches is also a much less intimidating and much more effective way to help develop students' oral communication skills. Instead of having one student speak to twenty-five classmates, you can have five students speak to four classmates. This enables more speeches, more practice, and more feedback.

Chapter 13

Questions and Discussions

This chapter describes strategies and techniques for creating effective classroom discussions. Classroom discussions enhance learning by (a) helping students to clarify, apply, and manipulate ideas and extend their thinking; (b) allowing teachers to see how students are processing new concepts, so they can adjust instruction accordingly; (c) enabling students to hear the thinking of other students; and (d) providing opportunities for students to participate and be actively engaged in the learning experience.

PLANNING DISCUSSIONS

Thoughtful planning is the first step in creating effective discussions. The questions should be designed to align with your lesson purpose and inserted into your lesson plan where they will be asked. However, having questions prepared does not preclude you from being flexible and spontaneous. It is common to prepare a set of questions and then to deviate once you get into the flow of the lesson. Also, if a question or topic seems to be creating an interesting discussion, allow students the freedom to explore it. This often leads to powerful, incidental learning experiences.

Preparing Questions

Two tips for designing effective questions. First, always test questions out on yourself first. If you have trouble answering it, chances are that students will be confused and have trouble answering it as well.

Second, try to include an equal number of low- and high-level questions. Bloom's Taxonomy (1956) can be used to help in creating questions at different levels (see figure 13.1). Knowledge and comprehension represent lower levels of thinking. Application and above represent higher levels of thinking. Use the action words associated with each level to design your questions.

One of the problems with using only low-level questions for discussions is that there is a tendency to fall into an IRE pattern. Here the teacher *initiates* the question, the students *respond*, and the teacher then *evaluates* that response (Cazden, 1998; Lukinsky & Schachter, 1998). IRE question patterns make the discussion feel more like an interrogation. The following is an example of an IRE discussion pattern:

Teacher: Students, what's the capital of Canada?

Student: Toronto.

Teacher: No.

Student: Montreal.

Teacher: No.

Student: Ottawa.

Teacher: Right. And which providence has the largest population?

Student: Quebec.

Teacher: No.

Student: Alberta.

Teacher: No.

Student: Ontario

Teacher: Yes. And what's the. . .

If your role becomes that of an evaluator or arbitrator of truth in a discussion, creative thinking and the free flow of ideas will be stymied. One way to avoid IRE question patterns is to include questions for which you do not know the answer.

1. Knowledge. Recalls facts or remembers previously learned material. *Knowledge level operations* -- define, describe, identify, list, match, name, tell, describe, show, label, collect, examine, tabulate, quote, duplicate, memorize, recognize, relate, recall, repeat, reproduce, or state.
2. Comprehension. Grasps the meaning of material. *Comprehension level operations* -- interpret, explain, summarize, convert, defend, distinguish, estimate, generalize, rewrite, contrast, predict, associate, distinguish, estimate, differentiate, discuss, extend, classify, discuss, express, indicate, locate, recognize, report, restate, review, select, or translate.
3. Application. Uses learned material in a new situation. *Application level operations* -- apply, change, compute, demonstrate, operate, show, use, solve, calculate, complete, illustrate, examine, modify, relate, change, classify, experiment, dramatize, employ, illustrate, interpret, operate, practice, schedule, sketch, or write.
4. Analysis. Breaks things down into parts in order to understand, organize, or clarify. *Analysis level operations* -- identify parts, distinguish, diagram, outline, relate or associate, break down, discriminate, subdivide, analyze, separate, order, explain, connect, classify, arrange, divide, select, explain, infer, analyze, appraise, calculate, categorize, compare, contrast, criticize, differentiate, discriminate, distinguish, examine, experiment, question, or test.
5. Synthesis. Puts parts together to form a new whole. *Synthesis level operations* -- combine, compose, create, design, rearrange, integrate, modify, substitute, plan, invent, formulate, prepare, generalize, or rewrite.
6. Evaluation. Uses a given criteria to determine the value of a thing or quality of a product or performance. *Evaluation level operations* -- appraise, criticize, compare and contrast, support, conclude, discriminate, find main points, explain, infer, deduce, assess, decide, rank, grade, test, measure, recommend, convince, select, judge, explain, discriminate, support, argue, choose compare, defend, estimate, judge, predict, rate, select, value, or evaluate.

Figure 13.1   Action words for Bloom's Taxonomy

VALUING RESPONSES

Students should never be made to feel inferior for responding to a question or participating in a class discussion. All responses should be valued. But what if a student says something that is obviously wrong or off the point? How do you value that kind of response? Acknowledge without evaluating (AWE). The following are some AWE examples:

"Interesting."
"There's a unique perspective."
"There's an idea I haven't heard before."
"Tell us why you think that way?"
"Sounds like you're doing some thinking."

The point is effective class discussions should be places to share insights and explore ideas. They should not turn into contests or quiz shows.

Also, nonverbal communication demonstrate that you value and are processing student's responses. Always look directly at the student who is speaking. Nod, smile, or give some sort of nonverbal or verbal prompt that shows you are listening. Example: "Yes." "I see." "Okay." You can also do *a sounds-like*. Here you rephrase and provide a brief overview of the student's point. For example:

"Sounds like you think the voting restrictions should be eliminated."
"Sounds like you liked the part in the story where Dorothy killed the witch."
"Sounds like you have some very strong feelings on this subject."

WAIT TIME AND PROCESSING

A common discussion mistake is to ask a question and then immediately call on a student or else to immediately provide the answer when there is no response. We may be uncomfortable with silence initially; however, it can enhance learning by allowing time for processing and reflection (Good & Brophy, 1995; Jensen, 2000). The period of silence after a question is asked and before a student answers is called wait time (Sternberg & Williams, 2010). Wait time gives all students a chance to think and respond. Even if hands go up immediately, you should wait five to seven seconds before calling on a student. Count silently to yourself to ensure you are providing adequate wait time. When asking complex or high-level questions, prove additional wait time for processing and reflection (seven to fifteen seconds).

Providing Time to Process Answers

The four strategies here enable students to process and think before they answer a question or engage in a discussion.

Journal or thinking paper. Have students write their responses or list ideas in a journal or on a piece of paper before beginning the discussion. As an example, Ms. Brady said to her 7th grade class, "Today I'd like to hear your ideas on having separate math and science classes for boys and girls. In your journal, list at least two ideas why you think it might be a good idea, a bad idea, or maybe both." As ideas were shared during the class discussion, students were encouraged, to add to their lists if they heard interesting or important ideas they liked. At the end of the class, students had several ideas to use to write a short position paper with supporting ideas or give a Small group speeche.

Preview questions. Ask a question or give a discussion prompt well before the discussion begins. For example, in his lesson on dragons in literature, Mr. Gonkowski said to his 4th grade class, "In just a minute I'm going to ask you to describe a dragon, so start thinking about it now." He began the lesson. When it came to share ideas, students had had time to think about dragons.

Neighbors. Before opening up a question for classroom discussion, have students turn to a neighbor and share their thoughts. Sometimes it works best to provide a bit of structure in this. For example, Ms. Garoppolo said to her 3rd grade class, "*In chapter 3 of our story, Billy Marble was captured by space aliens. Turn to your neighbor and share why you think the aliens selected Billy. I'll be calling on people in just a minute.*"

Small groups. Before engaging in a large group discussion, allow students to first have a discussion in small groups. For example, in his 11th-grade class, Mr. Edelman asked the question, "Should mixed martial arts (MMA) be banned?" He moved students into groups. When he saw the energy in the small groups starting to wane, he called them back and opened up the discussion to a large group.

T-TALKS

In classroom discussions, there is always a danger that the voices of a few people will dominate. The T-talk is a discussion strategy that enables all students to express their ideas. It also enhances discussions and allows for multiple viewpoints to be expressed. With adaptation, it can be used in kindergarten through high school. These are the steps:

1. Design a dualistic statement that reflects lesson content, assigned reading, or current events. A dualistic statement is one with which students have to either agree or disagree. For example: "*Mixed martial arts should be banned.*" "*All citizens should be required to vote.*" "*All high school students should be required to take a parenting class.*" "*The voting age should be lowered.*" "*Reading class should be in the afternoon instead of the morning.*" "*There should be a moment of silence every day in our school.*" "*School uniforms should be required.*" "*Dick should take Sally to the party.*" "*Jane should put Spot to sleep.*" These are all dualistic statements of which students can either support or not.

2. In pairs, students create a T-chart on a sheet of paper (see figure 13.2). On the T-chart, the pair lists a minimum of two ideas to support each side of the statement, regardless of what they actually think. At this stage, partners should not know each other's position. This usually takes about five minutes.

3. Each pair then combines with another pair to form a small group. Members share their ideas on both sides of the issue and identify their position. The group's task then is to try to reach a consensus. This is where most of the discussion occurs. There will be times when a consensus cannot be reached. When this occurs, the group may need to revise the dualistic statement or simply agree to disagree. All members will get a chance to describe their individual ideas later during class discussion or in their journals.

Agree	Disagree
1.	1.
2.	2.
3.	3.

Figure 13.2 T-Talk

4. At the end of the small group session, one speaker from each quad shares the group's conclusion. The speaker has one minute to share their group's position along with at least two reasons to support the group's new statement. Example: "*Our group believes. . . because (a) . . . and (b) . . .*"

5. The issue is opened for class discussion.

6. To make this a writing activity, students can describe their individual opinions in a blog, learning log, short paper, discussion site, or some other form.

T-Talks with Young Students

T-talks can be adapted for use with younger students in the primary grades by using it in large group. Here, the teacher records all of the students' ideas on a large chart or screen. Steps 2, 3, and 4 discussed in the previous section are skipped. For example, in her 1st grade classroom, Ms. Hightower used the dualistic statement: "School hours should be change to 12:00 to 6:00 PM." She helped students think of ideas on both sides of the issue. In this way, she was modeling a critical thinking skill, support-a-statement. As ideas were presented, she wrote them down on a Smart Board screen. Finally, she called on students to share their thoughts using one or two ideas from the board.

FINAL WORD

Classroom discussions enhance learning and can be used with all subject areas at all levels. However, effective discussions do not happen by accident; you need to plan and prepare. This is often a matter of designing three to five questions that align with the lesson's purpose. This ensures that your questions are purposeful instead of being used just to get students to talk. Also, T-talks can be used to create structure and to ensure that all participate.

Part V

PEDAGOGICAL STRATEGIES TO ENHANCE AND EXTEND LEARNING

This section contains seven chapters describing a variety of pedagogical strategies to enhance and extend learning. These include the following:

- Critical and creative thinking skills
- Using Bloom's taxonomy to create activities and assignments
- Learning contracts
- Agendas
- Tiered assignments
- Universal design for learning
- Learning stations
- Learning centers
- Using multiple intelligence (MI) theory to enhance learning
- Preparing online lessons

Chapter 14

Thinking Skills

If we want students to be proficient thinkers and to master complex cognitive processes, we must teach them how. Teaching thinking skills and embedding them across the curriculum can be used toward this end.

DEFINING OUR TERMS

A *thinking skill* is any cognitive process broken down into a set of steps which are then used to guide thinking (Johnson, 2000). For example, inference is a common cognitive process identified in many academic standards. To infer one must integrate observed clues with background knowledge in order to make an informed conjecture. This cognitive process can be made into a thinking skill by breaking it into the following steps: (a) identify the question or point of inference, (b) identify what is known or observed, (c) identify related knowledge that is relevant, and (d) make a reasoned guess based on b and c. This process can then be taught explicitly.

Thinking skills are different from *high-level thinking*. High-level thinking is any cognitive process that places high demands on the thinking and sorting of data taking place in short-term memory. Students do not benefit from simply being asked to engage in high-level thinking tasks unless first given explicit instruction. For example, a teacher could ask students to compare and contrast Harry Potter to Dorothy in the *Wizard of Oz*. Students who are already adept at this high-level thinking task might be able to do this easily while other students would probably become frustrated. Unfortunately, this is what often happens under the guise of thinking skills "instruction." Teachers simply present high-level tasks without any instruction. When this occurs, there is no actual teaching, very little learning, and a great deal of student frustration.

Thinking skills instruction, on the other hand, makes learning this cognitive process simple by making it a thinking skill. If students are to be able to compare and contrast, you must first break this cognitive process into the following steps: (a) look at the whole, (b) find the similarities, (c) find the differences, and (d) describe the whole in terms of similarities and differences. Then, teach it using direct instruction. With instruction, high-level thinking becomes relatively easy. This is the major premise of thinking skills instruction: Complicated things are made easy by breaking them into parts and teaching them explicitly.

THINKING SKILLS INSTRUCTION

Thinking skills should be taught using direct instruction (see chapter 7), and thinking frames. A thinking frame is a visual representation of the cognitive process broken down into specific steps (see table 14.1). These can be constructed in poster form and placed in the classroom for teaching and easy review.

Like any new skill, mastery of a thinking skill does not occur after a single encounter. It takes regular practice and review for students to learn and to be able to use it independently. Embedding thinking skills throughout the curriculum provides the necessary context for practice and mastery and enhances learning by enabling students to interact with content at deeper levels.

CRITICAL AND CREATIVE THINKING

Critical thinking is a type of thinking that converges on a single thought or entity. Here, one must organize, analyze, or evaluate information. The opposite of critical thinking is *creative thinking*. This is thinking that

Table 14.1   Examples of thinking frames

Infer	*Compare and Contrast*
1. Identify the question or point of inference.	1. Look at the whole.
2. Identify what is known or observed.	2. Find the similarities.
3. Identify related knowledge that is relevant.	3. Find the differences.
4. Make a reasoned guess based on b and c.	4. Describe in terms of similarities and differences.

diverges from a single point or entity. Here, one must generate, synthesize, find alternatives, adapt, substitute, or elaborate. Each of these cognitive processes could become thinking skills if they were broken into parts and taught explicitly.

Thinking Frames: Critical Thinking Skills

The thinking frames for eight critical thinking skills are outlined in figure 14.1. Each of these can be used to design activities and assignments.

Inferring: Go beyond the available information to identify what may reasonably be true. Thinking Frame 1. Identify what is known. 2. Identify similar situations or important knowledge. 3. Make a reasonable guess based on 1 and 2.	**Decision Making:** Examine the options and alternatives in order to decide on a course of action. Thinking Frame 1. Identify the problem or decision. 2. Generate decision options. 3. Evaluate costs and rewards of options. 4. Make a choice based on the above.
Compare and Contrast: Find similarities and differences between/among two or more items. Thinking Frame 1. Look at all items. 2. Find the similarities. 3. Find the differences. 4. Conclude and describe.	**Ordering:** Arrange events, concepts, or items in sequential order based on a criterion. Thinking Frame 1. Look at or define a criterion. 2. Look at the whole. 3. Arrange items within the whole according to the criterion. 4. Describe the whole in terms of the new order.
Analyze: Break an item or event down into its component parts. Thinking Frame 1. Look at the item or event. 2. Identify important parts. 3. Describe each part. 4. Describe the whole in terms each part	**Evaluation/Critique:** Make a formal critique based on a set of criteria. Thinking Frame 1. Look at or define a criterion. 2. Look at the subject. 3. Compare the subject to the criterion. 4. Describe the subject relative to the criterion.
Supporting a Statement: Use appropriate reasons, detail, or examples to support a statement, idea, or conclusion. Thinking Frame 1. Make a statement or claim. 2. Gather information/data to support the statement. 3. Organize the information. 4. Describe the original statement in terms of the new information.	**Creating Groups:** (inductive analysis) Impose order on a field by identifying and grouping common themes or patterns. Thinking Frame 1. Look at the whole. 2. Identify reoccurring items, themes, or patterns. 3. Arrange into groups. 4. Describe the whole in terms of groups.

Figure 14.1   Critical thinking skills

Thinking Frames: Creative Thinking Skills

The thinking frames for seven creative thinking skills are outlined in figure 14.2. Each of these can also be used to design activities and assignments.

Fluency: Generate as many ideas as possible without evaluating. Thinking Frame 1. Look at the idea or problem. 2. Do not worry about good or bad ideas. 3. Add as many ideas as quickly as you can. Flexibility: Create a variety of different approaches. Thinking Frame 1. Look at the original. 2. Find other ways for it to be used, solved, or applied. Elaboration: Embellish an original idea. Thinking Frame 1. Look at the idea. 2. Add things to it to make it better or more interesting. Originality: Create new ideas that are unusual or unique. Thinking Frame 1. Find an idea or problem. 2. Think of solutions or applications that nobody else has thought of before.	Integrate: Connect, combine, or synthesize two or more things to form a new whole. Thinking Frame 1. Look at all things. 2. Select interesting or important parts from each. 3. Combine to describe a new whole. Brainstorming Web: Create a web to generate ideas relative to a given topic. Thinking Frame 1. Look at the original ideas. 2. Analyze to identify 2-5 related ideas for subheadings. 3. Brainstorm to generate ideas for each subheading. 4. Describe. Generating Relationships: The student will find related items or events. Thinking Frame 1. Look at the item or event. 2. Generate attributes. 3. Find items or events with similar or related attributes. 4. Describe the relationship.

Figure 14.2   Thinking frames for creative thinking skills

THINKING SKILLS IN READING

This section demonstrates how thinking skills can be embedded within a curriculum. In his 6th grade reading class, Mr. Williams used thinking skills to create activities and assignments. They were reading the book *Harry Potter and the Sorcerer's Stone* (Rowling, 1997).

• **Fluency, creating groups, and analysis**. For a postreading activity, Mr. Williams' students generated (Fluency) a list of interesting or important events that had occurred in the story. These were recorded and inductive analysis was used to create groups (Creating Groups). The events in the story were then described in terms of groups and numbers within each group. Later, a table was created to organize these data. Individual chapters were then analyzed (Analysis) using the groups.

• **Ordering**. After reading a chapter, students worked in small groups to identify eight to ten important events. Students then organized the events in order of importance to the story from most important to least (Ordering) (see table 14.2).

• **Creative problem solving**. In chapter 10, Harry, Ron, and Hermione encounter a huge, dangerous troll in one of the corridors of the castle. Mr. Williams asked his students to use CPS to determine what could they do to solve this problem. This led to a wide variety of solutions. Students displayed their ideas on a bulletin board along with diagrams or necessary explanations.

Table 14.2   Orderizer

Generate a List	Put Them in Order
	1.
	2.
	3.
	4.

• **Elaboration**. As a postreading activity, Mr. Williams had his students imagine a character, event, scene, or item found in the chapter. In their reading logs, they were asked to describe interesting details not contained in the text. As well, students were given a sentence from the chapter. They were asked to add details or descriptive adjectives to make the sentence more interesting.

• **Web and brainstorm**. As a postreading activity, students created webs to describe the interesting or important events in that chapter (see figure 14.3). This is also an example of the thinking skill *Analyze* as students had to break the whole into its component parts and describe it. This technique was used instead of comprehension worksheets.

• **Compare and contrast**. Mr. Williams used the comparison chart in figure 14.4 to help his students make the following kinds of comparisons during the reading of this book: (a) the beginning of the book to the end, (b) Harry in chapter 1 to Harry in chapter 17, (c) Harry to another story character, (d) Harry to someone students know, (e) a character in the story to the student, (f) an event in the story to an event in students' lives, or (g) this story to another story.

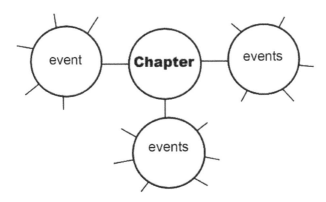

Figure 14.3   Web and brainstorm

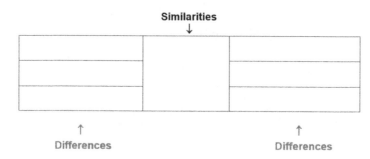

Similarities
↓

↑
Differences

↑
Differences

Conclusions or Ideas:

Figure 14.4   Comparison chart

At one point, he asked students to compare *Harry Potter and the Sorcerer's Stone* to similar stories. This lead naturally to discussions about genre. After talking about heroes and lead characters, students then decided to compare Luke from *Star Wars* to Dorothy from the *Wizard of Oz* (see figure 14.5).

• **Generate relationships**. To make personal connections, Mr. Williams asked students describe events or feelings from their lives that were similar to those found in the story or chapter. Example: In chapter 16, Harry had to go through the trapdoor and face danger. He was afraid. Mr. Williams had students write in their reading logs to describe one of the following: (a) a

Luke Skywalker from *Star Wars*	**things that are the same**	Dorothy Gale from *The Wizard of Oz*
a boy	both are teenagers	a girl
happens in the future	both live with aunt and uncle	happens in the past
evil character is male	both confront evil	evil character is female
in space	both find a magical power	on earth
	both have friends who help	
	both have creatures or animals talk	
Obi-Wan Kenobi	both have wise helping characters	Glinda the Good Witch

Figure 14.5   Comparison chart

time when you were afraid or (b) a time when you had to do something you didn't want to.

• **Infer**. Mr. Williams asked the following types of inference questions: "What might have happened in chapter 16 if Harry had failed?" Or, "How do you think Harry will be treated when he goes back to live with the Dursleys?" Students used information found in the story along with their own knowledge to make inferences about things not described. An Infer-O-Gram was used as a graphic organizer here (see figure 14.6).

• **Analyze**. At various points, students were asked to break the story or specific chapters into component parts and describe them. For example, students were asked to describe (a) important story events found in the beginning, middle, and end of the story or chapter; (b) the good, bad, and inauspicious story or chapter events, or (c) real things, possible things, and imaginary things found in the story or chapter. At times, Mr. Williams also asked students to decide how the story might best be broken into parts and how each part might be best described.

• **Supporting a statement**. Here, students were asked to use clues or sentences found in the story to support a statement (see figure 14.7).

Examples: In this story, students looked for clues to support the following the statements: (a) Hermione likes Ron, (b) Professor Snape is evil, (c) Harry is resourceful, or (d) Harry is a hero (see textbox 14.1).

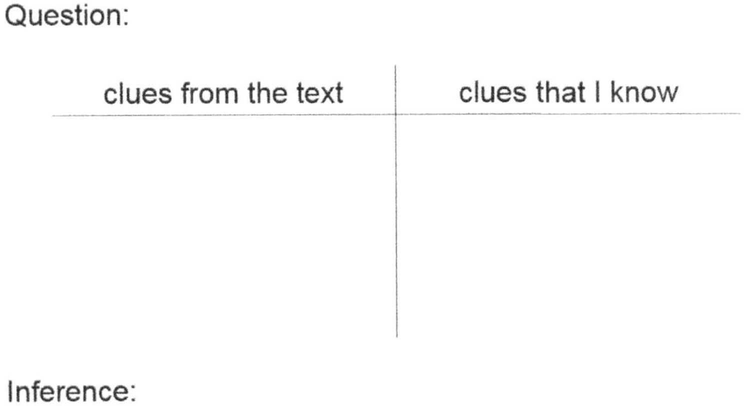

Question:

clues from the text	clues that I know

Inference:

Figure 14.6   Infer-O-Graph

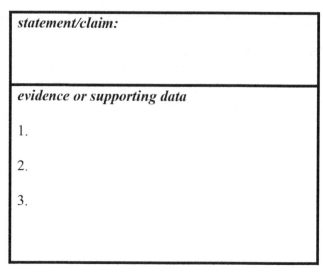

Figure 14.7   Supporting a statement

Topic Statement: Harry is a hero.

Supporting Ideas:

1. He is good at playing Quidditch.
2. He solves problems.
3. He fights evil.
4. He does things even when he is afraid.
5. He never gives up.

Textbox 14.1 Support statement

• **Evaluation/Critique**. Students were first asked to generate criteria for a good book, then use these criteria to rate the book (see figure 14.8). Students were then asked to rate this book on each of these criteria. Their criteria were also used to make comparisons with other books.

FINAL WORD

This chapter defined thinking skills as any cognitive process broken down into specific parts or steps. Thinking skills should be taught like any other skill, and the elements of effective skills instruction found in chapter 7 along

Criterion	Rating
Interesting or fun characters.	
Includes or uses magic.	
Interesting adventures.	
The story is imaginative.	

Key: 5 = very high, 4 = high, 3 = average, 2= low, 1 = very low

Figure 14.8   Evaluation

with thinking frames. Thinking skills can be used across the curriculum to design activities and assignments.

Chapter 15

Bloom's Taxonomy for Assignments and Activities

BLOOM'S TAXONOMY

Bloom's taxonomy of thinking was used in chapter 13 to design discussion questions. It will be used in chapter 17 to created tiered assignments. This chapter demonstrates how use Bloom's taxonomy to design assignments and activities.

Six Categories and Two Levels of Thinking

Bloom's taxonomy identifies six different kinds of thinking (Ormrod, 2012). These six categories can be separated into two levels: less complex thinking and more complex thinking. Being able to know or comprehend things is considered less-complex thinking (next section). These cognitive operations generally require less space in working memory and fewer component parts when compared to applying, analyzing, synthesizing, or evaluating things. Thus said, this is a taxonomy of thinking; not a hierarchy. A taxonomy is simply a system for classification. Even though the term "levels" is often used to describe each of the six types of thinking, there are really only two levels.

Less Complex Cognitive Operations

- **Knowledge.** Students recall facts or remembers previously learned material.

  - Knowledge level operations—define, describe, identify, list, match, name, tell, describe, show, label, collect, examine, tabulate, quote, duplicate, memorize, recognize, relate, recall, repeat, reproduce, or state.

- **Comprehension.** Students grasp the meaning of material. This assumes that there is some level of meaningful learning.

  - Comprehension level operations—interpret, explain, summarize, convert, defend, distinguish, estimate, generalize, rewrite, contrast, predict, associate, distinguish, estimate, differentiate, discuss, extend, classify, discuss, express, indicate, locate, report, restate, review, select, or translate.

Textbox 15.1

Describing the cognitive operations related knowledge and comprehension as less complex thinking is not meant to devalue this kind of thinking. This type of thinking is necessary in encoding and then being able to use and apply new information. However, when this is the only type of thinking used for activities, assignments, and discussions, this leads to low (less complex) levels of learning as students are not able to manipulate concepts deeply. As well, the activities using these cognitive operations are not very interesting. Sadly, this is type of thinking found on most "comprehension" worksheets in reading and study guides in other subject areas.

More Complex Cognitive Operations

- **Application.** Students use or apply learned material in a new situation.

  - Application level operations—apply, change, compute, demonstrate, operate, show, use, solve, calculate, complete, illustrate, examine, modify, relate, change, classify, experiment, dramatize, employ, illustrate, interpret, operate, practice, schedule, sketch, or write.

- **Analysis.** Students break things down into parts in order to understand, organize, or clarify.

  - Analysis level operations—identify parts, distinguish, diagram, outline, relate or associate, break down, discriminate, subdivide, analyze, separate, order, explain, connect, classify, arrange, divide, select, explain, infer, analyze, appraise, calculate, categorize, compare, contrast, criticize, differentiate, discriminate, distinguish, examine, experiment, question, or test.

- **Synthesis.** Students put parts together to form a new whole.

  - Synthesis level operations—combine, compose, create, design, rearrange, integrate, modify, substitute, plan, invent, formulate, prepare, generalize, or rewrite.

- **Evaluation.** Using a given criteria, students determine the value of a thing or quality of a product or performance.

  - Evaluation level operations—appraise, criticize, compare and contrast, support, conclude, discriminate, find main points, explain, infer, deduce, assess, decide, rank, grade, test, measure, recommend, convince, select, judge, explain, discriminate, support, argue, choose, defend, estimate, judge, predict, rate, select, value, or evaluate.

Textbox 15.2

CREATING ACTIVITIES AND ASSIGNMENTS

So how do you use this taxonomy? Simply use the action words in Bloom's taxonomy to help you design activities and assignments. You need never rely on a teacher's manual or activity book ever again.

Literacy Class: The Little Pigs

Ms. Allen's 5th grade class was reading the original versions of common fairy tales. She created the following activities for *The Three Pigs*.

- **Knowledge.** Describe how the wolf got into the house of the third pig.
- **Comprehension.** Create a story map that shows the events that happened in this story.
- **Application.** Create a one-minute mime drama that shows how the wolf tried to get into the third pig's house and what happened.
- **Analysis**. Using a Web-of-Comparison, compare and contrast *The Three Pigs* and *Little Red Riding Hood*.
- **Evaluation**. Define four elements of a good story. Rate *The Three Pigs* on each element (evaluation).
- **Analysis.** Using the four elements of a good story (discussed earlier), rate *Little Red Riding Hood* and compare the two stories.
- **Evaluation.** Compare and contrast, *The Three Pigs* to *Little Red Riding Hood* to find similarities and differences.
- **Synthesis.** Create a happy ending to this story in which the wolf does not get hurt.

Science Class: Amphibians

Ms. Nelson was teaching her 3rd grade class about amphibians as part of her science unit related to Living Systems (see chapter 5). The following are examples of ten different activities or assignments based on the action words from Bloom's taxonomy that she designed for use with her amphibian lessons:

• **Knowledge**. Students were given pictures of the life cycle of an amphibian and asked to put them in the correct order.
• **Knowledge**. Students were asked to identify and label the defining attributes of an amphibian.
• **Comprehension**. Students were presented with pictures of reptiles, amphibians, fish, and water mammals. They were asked to put them into the correct categories.
• **Application**. Students created and performed a creative dramatics skit showing an amphibian changing from tadpole with gills to adult with lungs.
• **Analysis**. Students examined several species of frogs and used inductive analysis to put them into groups according to physical characteristics. The same was done with toads and salamanders.
• **Analysis**. Students examined a variety of species of frog and the environment in which each was found. They identified physical characteristics that were necessary for each to survive and thrive.
• **Synthesis**. Students used poetry to describe an amphibian of their choice.
• **Synthesis**. Using only words found in their textbook, students created poetry on topics of their choice.
• **Synthesize**. Students designed a creative dramatics presentation that portrayed the life cycle of a frog.
• **Evaluation**. Compare and contrast how amphibians warm and cool their bodies, to reptiles, mammals, and birds.

FINAL WORD

Benjamin Bloom originally created this taxonomy to be used to design educational objectives. However, the value in the taxonomy is not in writing lesson plan objectives. Instead, the action words for each level can be used to design activities and assignments.

Chapter 16

Learning Contracts

A *learning contract* is a written agreement between a student or students and the teacher that specifies what will be learned, how it will be learned, how learning will be demonstrated, and the time frame for completion of the learning experience (Johnson, 2009; Tomlinson, 1995). They are used to create open-ended, student-centered learning experiences. They can be used as well to differentiate the curriculum for students of differing abilities levels. Learning contracts come in various forms and should be adapted to meet the needs, interest, and abilities of students.

TEACHER AND STUDENT-SELECTED LEARNING OBJECTIVES

Presented in this section are (a) a description of the steps used to design a learning contract to meet teacher-selected goals and objectives, (b) an example of a 7th grade learning contract, and (c) directions for adapting the learning contract for student-selected learning objectives.

The Steps

These are the steps for designing a learning contract:

1. **Identify specifically what you want students to learn**. Learning contracts can be used to (a) meet current curricular goals, (b) enhance curriculum content, (c) expand upon or examine related content, or (d) discover things of importance and interest to the student. Each of these outcomes has its merits; no one should be used exclusively.

2. **Assemble or identify learning resources.** This could include but should not be limited to books, articles, magazines, computer programs, websites, community experts, or videos. For younger students, you will need to gather these sources for them. Older students can begin to find their own resources.

3. **Decide how students will demonstrate their learning.** As you can see later, there are a variety of ways in which students can demonstrate their learning. These demonstrations are found on a continuum consisting of structured objective exams, written reports, and class presentations on one end; to visual art, websites, mock interviews, and creative dramatics on the other end.

4. **Design grading criteria.** A variety of checklists and rubrics can be used for a learning contract; however, it is always best to keep these simple. Keep in mind, the goal is not to measure and assess; rather, for students to learn. For older students, grading a learning contract is appropriate at times; however, for younger students this is rarely the case.

Grading criteria for a learning contract

CRITERIA   Learning contracts are designed around the following criteria:

- **Responsibility:** In fulfilling your learning contract: (a) you used your time wisely, (b) you met your goals for check-up dates and completion dates, and (c) you asked questions when needed.
- **Knowledge:** Your demonstration of knowledge (a) is interesting and informative, (b) fully addresses learning objectives, (c) uses correct knowledge, and (d) uses complete knowledge.
- **Thinking:** The demonstration of knowledge (a) meets learning objectives, (b) expresses knowledge accurately, and (c) shows the learner's thinking.
- **Communication:** (when appropriate) The demonstration of knowledge (a) is free of mistakes and of high quality; (b) is clear, logical, and organized; (c) meets time or length parameters; and (d) is interesting, creative, or expresses important ideas.

Textbox 16.1

5. **Identify check-up dates and dates for completion.** Check-up dates are agreed upon times when the teacher and students check on the progress being made. The completion date is when students will demonstrate their learning.

Example

Ms. Nelson's 7th grade history class was studying economic expansion from 1792 to 1861. The focus was on four new technologies that transformed the U.S. economy and society: the cotton gin, power loom, steam engine, and the railroad. Instead of the usual lecture, Ms. Nelson decided to use learning contracts. Students were assigned to small groups. Next, each group drew for the technology that they would study. After a brief small group discussion, Ms. Nelson met with each group to agree upon a contract for learning.

Contract for learning

I.   What will you learn or learn about?
You will learn about (cotton gin, power loom, steam engine, rail road). You will do the following:

1. Describe the defining features of the invention.
2. Describe what was used before.
3. Describe the change the occurred after.
4. Describe three other interesting or important things.

II.   How will you learn? (check all the applied)

__ books
__ websites
___ interview experts
___ magazines
___ learn from others: peer, parent, or expert
___ observation
___ survey or interview
___ other

III.   How will you work?

___ individually ___ pairs ___ small groups

IV.   How will you demonstrate your learning?

___ poster session
___ demonstration
___ poetry
___ objective exams
___ mock interview
___ create a website
___ PowerPoint presentation

___ class speech/presentation
___ visual art
___ creative drama or reenactment
___ write a story (realistic fiction)
___ write a story (nonfiction)
___ video documentary
___ write a report
___ other

V.   How should you be graded?
VI. Dates

First check-up date _____
Second check-up date _____
Completion date _____

Textbox 16.2

Once the contract was agreed upon, Ms. Nelson designed a checklist that included her grading criteria. This was presented to students before they began their contracted learning experience. Upon completion, the checklist was used as a basis for assessing their work. As students used class time to complete their contracts, Ms. Nelson's role became that of a coach, helping her students complete their agendas. Also, she used observations of her students as the basis of short mini-lesson for both large group and small groups. In other words, if she noticed students struggling with a skill or concept, she was able to use a meaningful context to provide short bits of very direct and explicit instruction.

Student-Selected Learning Objectives

Learning contracts can also be designed to enable students to choose the topic to be studied. Choice is one of the most powerful factors in creating intrinsic motivation for learning. Typically, the topic students choose is related to a curriculum or area of study; however, there should be times when students should be given total freedom to choose their topic of study. The learning that takes place here goes beyond that associated with the topic of study. Students also learn about the process of asking a question and gathering data to answer the question.

The process used for designing and implementing this type of learning contract is similar to that is discussed earlier. The difference being that once students have identified a topic or area of interest, you will need to help them put it in the form of one or more questions. Well-defined questions help define students' learning goals and provides focus data collection. Also, the contract and grading criteria used here would be similar to those used that was discussed earlier.

GRADING CRITERIA

Demonstration of knowledge: (This is a description of how students demonstrated their knowledge.)

Key: √ = trait is present; √+ = trait is present to a greater degree;
  √- = trait is present to a lesser degree; # trait is not present

___1. Used time wisely.
___ 2. Met goals for check-up and completion dates.
___ 3. The presentation demonstrated knowledge of the learning objectives:
  ___ • Described the defining features of the invention.
  ___ • Described what was used before.
  ___ • Described the change the occurred after.
  ___ • Described three additional interesting or important things.
___ 4. The presentation was organized and showed student thinking.
___ 5. The presentation was interesting or expressed important ideas.

Figure 16.1   Grading criteria for contracted learning experience

Contract for student-selected learning objectives.

I.   What is your topic or area of interest?
II. What is/are your specific research question or questions.
III. How will you work?

___ individually ___ pairs ___ small groups

IV. How will you learn? (check all the applied)
__ books
__ websites
___ interview experts
___ magazines
___ learn from others: peer, parent, or expert.
___ observation
___ survey or interview
___ other.

V. How will you demonstrate your learning?
___ poster session
___ demonstration
___ poetry
___ objective exams
___ mock interview
___ create a website
___ PowerPoint presentation
___ class speech/presentation
___ visual art
___ creative drama or reenactment
___ write a story (realistic fiction)
___ write a story (nonfiction)
___ video documentary
___ write a report
___ other

VI. How should you be graded?
V. Dates

First check-up date _____
Second check-up date _____
Completion date _____

Textbox 16.3

AGENDAS

An agenda is a personalized list of tasks given to students (Tomlinson, 2001). The tasks should be designed to accommodate each students' abilities and interests. In a given class, there is apt to be several different agendas being used simultaneously, making it an effective tool to use in differentiating the curriculum for students of differing ability levels.

Depending on age, students are usually given from two days to two weeks to complete their individualized agendas.

GRADING CRITERIA

Demonstration of knowledge:

Key: √ = trait is present; √+ = trait is present to a greater degree;
√- = trait is present to a lesser degree;   # trait is not present

Learning contracts can be design around the following criteria:

___ 1. Used time wisely.
___ 2. Met goals for check-up and completion dates.
___ 3. Used data to answer the question/s.
___ 4. The presentation was organized and showed thinking.
___ 5. The presentation was interesting or expressed important ideas.

Figure 16.2   Checklist for contracted learning experience

	I	
Personal agenda for : _____		
Starting date: _____ Date for completion: _____		
Student and teacher initial after completion.	**Task**	**Special Instructions**
	With a partner, read the article, "Invention of the Steam Engine." Describe three interesting or important ideas.	Use reciprocal reading. Record the ideas in your learning log
	Look on the internet to find and describe three changes that occurred after the steam engine was invented.	What was it like before the steam engine? What are three changes that occurred. Record your ideas in your learning log.
	Listen to the vocabulary tape that defines and describes each of the following words: combustion, external combustion, piston, cylinder, steam, turbine, energy, boiler,	Write five interesting or creative sentences. Each sentence should contain at least one vocabulary word. Record your sentences in your learning log.
	Complete the two Steam Engine worksheets.	Check your answers and put them in your portfolio.
	Choose two vocabulary words to include for study for your weekly spelling. Add eight of your own words that you wish to study this week.	Record the words and the definitions in your learning log. Look them up in the dictionary to make sure they are spelled correctly.
	Look on the internet to find an interesting web site related to steam engines.	Work with a partner to complete the web site description sheet.

Figure 16.3   Example of an agenda for technologies and innovations: 1792–1861

FINAL WORD

Learning contracts and agendas are used to create open-ended, individualized, student-centered learning. The use of learning contracts can be used effectively in an inclusive, multilevel learning environment. And since students are not homogenous, standardized entities, all learning environments can be considered to be multilevel to some degree.

Chapter 17

Tiered Assignments and UDL

Humans are not standardized products. In most classrooms, it is very likely that some students are achieving two or more grade levels above grade level average and others are achieving two or more grade levels below grade level average. In these classrooms, you can expect to encounter students with different languages, learning styles, emotional needs, backgrounds, values, traditions, socioeconomic status, religions, cultures, and interests. Given this, it seems rather silly to think that you can serve up one common educational experience and expect to meet everybody's learning needs. Instead, some sort of differentiation is needed. This chapter describes two strategies for differentiating a curriculum to meet the varying learning needs of the students in your classroom: tiered assignments and Universal Design for Learning.

TIERED ASSIGNMENTS

A tiered assignment manipulates the same idea or input at different levels or tiers (Tomlinson, 2001). Here, the same lesson is presented to all students; however, the post-lesson activities or assignments are designed at differing levels of complexity. In this way, each student still comes away with important knowledge and at the same time is challenged at a level appropriate for his or her ability.

As shown in chapters 14 and 16, action words for the different cognitive operations in Bloom's taxonomy of thinking can be used to help design activities and assignments at differing levels. Since these have already been presented, an abbreviated version is used here for demonstration purposes.

Abbreviated Version of Bloom's Action Words

- Synthesis: compose, design, invent, create, construct, rearrange parts, imagine
- Evaluation: judge, rank, evaluate, critique, give opinion, order, defend
- Analysis: classify, categorize, compare, contrast, solve, break into parts
- Application: demonstrate, use, describe, map, chart, do, real life
- Comprehension: restate, give example, explain, summarize, translate, draw, diagram, response to question
- Knowledge: tell, recite, list, remember, define, locate, respond, remember

---

Textbox 17.1

Textbox 17.2 demonstrates how these can be used to create three levels of activities using the movie, *The Wizard of Oz.*

Tiered Assignment Example for Wizard of Oz

The Wizard of Oz.
   Select one of the following activities:

1. Describe one or more examples from the movie where Dorothy showed courage. Describe one or more examples from your life where you or somebody else showed courage.
2. List five criteria for a good fantasy or fairy tale. Evaluate the Wizard of Oz on these criteria, rating each from one to ten, with ten being the highest.
3. What common elements do you see in the following movies: *The Matrix, Star Wars: Episode I—The Phantom Menace, Wizard of Oz,* or other.

Textbox 17.2

When implementing tiered assignments, start with just two levels. When you feel comfortable with the process, you may want to use three levels. You would rarely need to use more than three levels. Most often, students are assigned or given an activity from one of the levels; however, you may also want to include times when students would be able to choose the type or level of activity or assignment.

UNIVERSAL DESIGN FOR LEARNING

This section describes the basic principles of Universal Design for Learning (UDL). UDL is an educational framework that guides the development and design of flexible, multilevel learning experiences (Woolfolk, 2015). It involves the following elements: content, input or instruction, and activity/assessment (CIA).

Content. This is the information that is provided to students. Content can be varied in terms of more complex or less complex. For example, instead of the regular chapter in the science textbook, provide alternative reading material that describes similar ideas at higher levels for high-ability learners and lower levels for students who are struggling learners.

Instruction or input. This is how information is provided to students. Differentiation can include the following:

- Recorded books
- Online mini-lectures created by the teacher
- Small group mini-lessons, instruction, or activities
- Independent programs
- Graphic organizers to make content more visual
- Guided notes
- Internet or video presentations
- Learning centers or stations
- Discovery learning

Activity and assessment. This is how students manipulate or use the information or skills. Differentiation here includes the following:

- Tiered instruction based on Bloom's taxonomy
- Cooperative learning activities
- Multiple intelligence activities
- Using thinking skills
- Problem-based learning
- Inquiry learning activities
- Creative dramatics

Differentiation here can also involve alternative ways for students to demonstrate their learning (see table 17.1).

Table 17.1   Alternative ways for students to demonstrate learning

• Small group speeches	• Weigh or measure	• Record an interview
• Journals/learning logs	• Plan and perform a	• Create a play
• Create graphic organizer	newscast	• Create a dance
or semantic map	• Design a crossword	• Make a commercial
• Create a poem	puzzle	• Use dance or mime to
• Put important items or	• Make a game or design	express an idea
events on a time line	a quiz show	• Create a rap song
• Plan and perform a	• Create a sculpture or	• Design a reading guide
newscast	painting	• Find related issues
• Do an interview show	• Create a radio drama	• Describe an idea using
• Design a crossword	• Create a bulletin board	numbers
puzzle	• Design a poster	• Design a crossword
• Describe multiple	• Design a survey	puzzle
viewpoints	• Design a web page	
• Write a newspaper article	• Engage in a T-talk	

FINAL WORD

In all classrooms, it is most likely that you will encounter students that have a wide range of interests, ways of thinking, and ability levels. Tiered assignments and UDL are two simple ways to differentiate a common curriculum to meet the needs of students of varying ability levels.

Chapter 18

Learning Stations and Learning Centers

This chapter examines two pedagogical strategies that can be used for both remediation and extension to focus on specific concepts of skills: learning stations and learning centers.

LEARNING STATIONS

Learning stations are designated places in the classroom used to practice, reinforce, or extend a skill or related set of skills (Johnson, 2009). They are used simultaneously with the whole class. Here the teacher designs short mini-lessons or activities for each station. Small groups of three to five students go to a station and work on the activity. On a common signal (classroom lights flashing or a bell), each small group rotates to the next station. This continues until the whole class has worked through all stations. Sometimes, it is appropriate to have a parent, paraprofessional, or older student assigned to a station to provide short bits of instruction. Depending on the age of the student and the number of stations, students should spend five to ten minutes at each station.

Example: Learning Stations

Mr. Baker was teaching students his 9th grade English class the basics of academic writing. He used learning stations in his classes whenever he noticed common issues in students' writing that needed to be addressed. Stations enabled him to give his students several quick mini-lessons during a single class period. Also, the conversation that occurred in small groups, enhanced learning.

On this day, Mr. Baker had identified eight problems that many students were having with their writing. He designed eight stations to practice or reinforce skills taught during the week. Each station included a very simple written review of the designated writing skill along with examples. Example: *Paragraphs are used to separate ideas. When you start a new idea, start a new paragraph*. Students were put in groups of three and four. To avoid chaos, each station used a form of cooperative learning in which specific roles were defined. The following stations were used:

Station 1—identify the paragraph. Students were given a paper that had a large blob of text without paragraphs. They were to mark on the text where they thought the new paragraphs should be started. They then moved to the computer that had the same unparagraphed text. They used their paper draft to create paragraphs and printed out the text. They compared their version to an edited version in which the correct paragraphs were included.

Station 2—identify the complete sentence. Students were given a paper that contained several sentences. Some of them were complete sentences, some of them were not. They were asked to identify the incomplete sentences and make them complete. They then compared their sentences to a version in which all the sentences were complete sentences.

Station 3—create groups. Students were presented with a sheet of paper containing a random list of ideas related to a writing topic. Using inductive analysis, students were to put the ideas into groups and create an outline with ordinate and subordinate points that could be used to write a rough draft.

Station 4—brainstorm ideas. Students were given a writing topic. At this station, they were asked to brainstorm ideas for the writing topic. If time, they were to look for possible groups to use to organize a draft.

Station 5—edit for precision. Students were given a paper that had sentences in which there were too many words. They were to look for words that could be removed in each sentence, or find more concise, precise ways of communicating the idea. They then moved to the computer, made the changes, and printed it out. They then compared their edited paper with a version containing very concise, precise academic writing.

Station 6—edit for consistency of tense. Students were presented with paragraphs in which there were inconsistent uses of tense. Students edited and made changes on paper, then compared their edits with a corrected version.

Station 7—edit for consistency of plurality. Students were presented with paragraphs in which there were inconsistent uses of plurality. Students edited and made changes on paper. Students edited and made changes on paper, then compared their edits with a corrected version.

Station 8—edit for colloquialisms or speech language. Students were presented with paragraphs containing what he called "speechisms" or nonacademic language. Students identified these on paper first, and then moved to the computer to make the changes. They then compared their edits with a corrected version.

Students were told they had seven minutes to complete the tasks at each station; however, Mr. Baker watched his students to get a sense of when to transition. He found that toward the end, students became more efficient and needed less time. Mr. Baker was working within the constraints of a fifty-minute class period. He realized that he might not be able to get students through all the stations in a single class period. Thus, he made this a two-day project.

LEARNING CENTERS

A *learning center* is a designated place in the classroom that contains activities or materials designed to reinforce or extend a skill or concept (Jarolimek, Foster, & Kellough, 2005). Unlike the learning station, students do not rotate. They spend all their time at one center. Also, learning centers are self-sufficient or mostly self-sufficient. Students should be able to go to a learning center and complete the activities without a great deal of additional instruction (unless it is being used for remediation).

Example: Learning Centers

Ms. Torres designed learning centers for her 2nd grade classroom that included activities to extend or apply information students learned in their science and social studies units. She also used learning centers to reinforce, apply, or extend skills related to math, reading, and writing. Throughout the year, she created interdisciplinary learning centers where she combined math, reading, and writing with other curriculum areas.

Learning centers should be fun and engaging. It is best to start with one or two learning centers where students can go after their other work is completed. However, this approach can give the impression that learning centers are merely keeping-busy-centers so use this sparingly. Other ways to use learning centers are described further:

• **Learning center day.** Here, students work in small groups at a single center for the entire class period. Once a week Ms. Torres has a learning center day where she sets up several centers in her room. Sometimes she allows groups to choose a center. Other times she designs and assigns learning centers to meet the needs or interests of students. In this way, she is able to differentiate the learning experience.

• **Remediation**. Learning centers can be used for remediation. Here a teacher, paraprofessional, or even an older student provides instruction and practice with a designated group of students. Instead of completing homework or other assignments, these students would receive instruction and guided practice in the learning center. Computers and computer programs can also be used here, but these should always be thoughtfully considered.

• **Open-ended learning centers.** The activities at these types of learning centers would require students to use creativity and problem-solving skills to design a product or performance or to solve a problem that is ill-structured. For example, students might be given a school or community problem to solve using CPS or MEA (see chapter 9). They could be given a moral dilemma or a values clarification activity (see chapter 29), or be asked to design a book cover for the book they are reading. They might create and perform a short drama, design a PowerPoint presentation, write a book review, create a poster, write an editorial, design a comic strip, write a script, record an instructional or persuasive video, or evaluate a website.

FINAL WORD

Learning stations and learning centers are both pedagogical strategies that can be used in kindergarten through graduate school in various forms. Learning stations are a series of mini-lessons created at specific locations in a class-room that are used to remediate or extend skills and concepts. Students spend five to ten minutes at a station in small groups and rotate through all stations during a given class period. Learning centers are places in the classroom used to remediate or extend skills and concepts. One student or small groups spend extended time here. With the learning center, there is no rotation.

Chapter 19

Using Multiple Intelligence Theory to Enhance Learning

This chapter looks at two influential multiple intelligence theories: Gardner's theory of multiple intelligence and Sternberg's triarchic theory of intelligence. These theories provide a basis for designing activities and assignments that employ different types of thinking.

GARDNER'S THEORY OF MULTIPLE INTELLIGENCE

Howard Gardner's book *Frames of Mind* (1993) defined intelligence as the ability to solve problems or create products that are valued within a culture. Gardner identified eight different intelligences, each of which involves different ways of thinking:

1. **Linguistic intelligence:** It is the ability to use words to describe or communicate ideas. Examples of occupations using this kind of thinking include writer, reporter or journalist, poet, debater, comedian, newscaster, public speaker, public relations, politician, editor, teacher, and professor.

2. **Logical-mathematical intelligence:** It is the ability to perceive patterns in numbers or reasoning, to use numbers effectively, or to reason well using analytic or deductive thinking. Examples of occupations using this kind of thinking include mathematician, scientist, researcher, accountant, computer programmer, statistician, logician, lawyer, doctor, and detective.

3. **Spatial intelligence:** It is the ability to perceive the visual-spatial world accurately (not get lost) and to transform it. Examples of occupations using this kind of thinking include artist or sculptor, set designer, hunter, guide, engineer, film animator, 3D simulator, interior decorator, and architect.

4. **Bodily-kinesthetic intelligence:** It is expertise in using or controlling one's body. Examples of occupations using this kind of thinking include athlete, yoga instructor, mime, and dancer.

5. **Musical intelligence:** It is the ability to recognize and produce rhythm, pitch, and timbre; to express musical forms; and to use music to express an idea. Examples of occupations using this kind of thinking include musician, composer, recording engineer, piano tuner, director, performer, and musical technician.

6. **Interpersonal intelligence:** It is the ability to perceive and appropriately respond to the moods, temperaments, motivations, and needs of other people. Inter means between. Interpersonal intelligence means between people. Examples of occupations using this kind of thinking include counselor, administrator, teacher, manager, coach, co worker, politician, group mediator, conflict-resolution specialist, pastor, psychologist, salesperson, and parent.

7. **Intrapersonal intelligence:** It is the ability to access one's inner life; to discriminate one's emotions, intuitions, and perceptions; and to know one's strengths and limitations. Intra means within. Intrapersonal intelligence means within the person. Examples of occupations using this kind of thinking include religious leader, actor, artist, writer, counselor, psychotherapist, writer, and philosopher.

8. **Naturalistic intelligence:** It is the ability to recognize and classify living things (plants, animals) as well as sensitivity to other features of the natural world (rocks, clouds). Examples of occupations using this kind of thinking: naturalist, botanist, gardener, geologist, hunter, scout or guide, farmer, and environmentalist.

Creating Multimodal Instruction Using MI Theory

Incorporating the varied types of thinking identified by Gardner's theory into lessons makes learning more multimodal and enables students to learn more deeply (Diaz-Lefebvre, 2006; Kornhaber, 2004). The actions words associated with each type of thinking can be used to help design activities and assignments.

Action words for Gardner's MI theory

1. Linguistic intelligence action words: speak, write, read, compose, create word pictures, narrate, describe
2. Logical-mathematical intelligence action words: deduce, if/then logic, when/then logic, puzzle, reason, figure, compute, calculate, analyze
3. Spatial intelligence action words: draw, diagram, illustrate, shape, sketch, create, design
4. Bodily-kinesthetic intelligence action words: move, dance, create shapes, mime, move

5. Musical intelligence action words: sing, play, use rhythms, create song, dance, hum, recognize sounds, use music, compose
6. Interpersonal intelligence action words: work with partner, work in small groups, share, talk, cooperative learning, listen, lead, direct, interact, decide, negotiate, compromise
7. Intrapersonal intelligence action words: make personal connections, imagine, intuit, associate emotions or experiences, emote, reflect, associate, remember, value, define, identify
8. Naturalistic intelligence action words: go outside, use natural things (this one is hard to do in a classroom).

Textbox 19.1

STERNBERG'S TRIARCHIC THEORY OF INTELLIGENCE

Another expanded view of intelligence is Robert Sternberg's (1996) triarchic theory of intelligence. This theory recognizes three types of thinking that work together to solve problems, create products, or enable outstanding performance: creative, evaluation, and pragmatic thinking. Creative thinking is the ability to generate ideas and make associations. Evaluative thinking is the ability to monitor executive processes and analyze and appraise ideas. And pragmatic thinking is the ability to recognize the context of the situation and adapt the idea to that context.

Three Types of Thinking in Sternberg's Triarchic Intelligence Theory

- **Generative thinking**. Generate many ideas, synthesize ideas, create original ideas, think outside the box, or utilize divergent thinking and inductive reasoning.
- **Evaluative thinking**. Evaluate ideas, analyze ideas, organize ideas, compare ideas, or utilize convergent thinking and deductive reasoning.
- **Pragmatic thinking**. Implement, apply, or adapt the ideas produced through generative and evaluative thinking to meet the demands of your particular situation.

Textbox 19.2

Students will learn more and learn more deeply if you include these three types of thinking in the questions, activities, and assignments in daily lessons and across the curriculum (Sternberg & Grigorenka, 2000). The actions words in table 19.1 can be used to assist in the design of these thinking.

Table 19.1   Action words for Sternberg's triarchic theory of intelligence

1. Generative thinking	2. Evaluative thinking	3. Pragmatic thinking
• Generate many ideas • Synthesize two or more ideas • Create original ideas • Find ideas that nobody else has considered • Utilize divergent thinking • Elaborate—add to ideas	• Evaluate ideas • Analyze ideas • Break thinking into parts • Organize ideas • Compare ideas • Critique ideas • Convergent thinking • Deductive reasoning	• Implement • Apply • Work out the bugs • Revise and reshape • Make idea fit the real • Adapt the ideas produced through generative and evaluative thinking to meet the demands of your particular situation

FINAL WORD

Gardner's Theory of Multiple Intelligence and Sternberg's Triarchic Intelligence Theory are both examples of expanded views of intelligence. The action words associated with each can be used to design questions, activities, and assignments. Using these enhances learning by making it more multimodal.

Chapter 20

Preparing Online Lessons and Presentations

THE ONLINE LESSONS

Effective online teaching is not simply an in-person teaching episode that has been recorded and slapped on the Internet. You must think, plan, and teach in ways that complement this new medium. The following are some general tips to consider when preparing online lessons and presentations.

Planning the Online Lesson

• **Know your audience.** There are real people out there. In preparing a lesson, know who you are teaching. What do they need to know? What do they not need to know? What links can be made from the known to the new? What level of complexity is appropriate?

• **Identify a purpose.** Just like all lessons, you must start with a purpose statement. Example: *Students will learn about* [*insert topic here*]. Everything that follows should be related to that purpose statement. Online lessons need to be shorter and more compact than an in-person lesson. Only include things that are directly related to your lesson purpose.

• **Create lessons that are short, briskly paced, and highly visual.** There are a many things competing for student's attention in an Internet environment. Large topics should be broken up into separate segments and included in separate lessons. Depending on your audience, online lessons should be between two and eight minutes. People will be more inclined to listen to and pay attention to a short, briskly paced, informative lesson then they are lessons that are ten minutes in duration or longer.

• **Use a PowerPoint, Prezi, or some other slide presentation**. A person simply talking to a camera is a very ineffective for an online lesson. Online lessons must be designed using slides and pictures. PowerPoint and Prezi (slides) enable you to include a variety of colors, font, and font size as well as movement and pictures.

• **Less is better than more**. Instead of trying to cover the complete topic, consider the main ideas. Consider what can be taught in a two- to eight-minute lesson. Learning is more effective when fewer things are addressed in depth than when many things are "covered" in a shallow way.

• **Use structure to carry your presentation.** Having structure for any type of lesson enhances your ability to teach effectively and students' ability to encode the new information. Create structure by identifying three to five subtopics. Use these to create an advanced organizer that shows the structure of what is to be covered in the lesson (see figure 20.1). During the lesson used various colored fonts and headings to highlight the structure.

Designing Your Slides

• **Use PowerPoint or Prezi slides to hold and organize ideas.** Include just enough words on your slides to hold and organize ideas as you are teaching. PowerPoint slides should not be used to transmit information. You are the information transmitter.

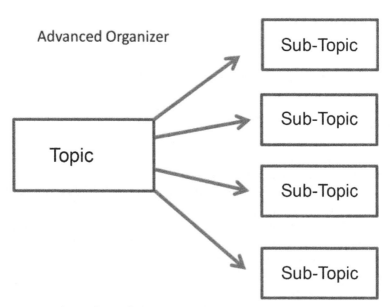

Figure 20.1   Advanced organizer

• **Use 24-point font or larger.** In most cases, do not use font smaller than 24-points for your slides. When designing lessons for younger children, larger font should be used.

• **Include no more than four sentences or ideas on a slide.** Two sentences or ideas per slide is ideal. This will keep things moving.

• **Use pictures, pictures, pictures.** This is a very visual medium. Include pictures to highlight your ideas. There should be a picture or a symbol on every slide to illustrate what you are teaching. Also, include colors on the background slides and font. This creates a multimodal presentation.

• **Use transition markers.** If you are transitioning from one subtopic to another, include a transition marker of some kind to let the student know you are moving to a different topic.

Teaching: The Performing Skills

• **Include your face if possible**. Most online recording programs include a video option that shows your face. If possible, use this. We communicate with our face and body language as well as our words. Also, seeing a face on the side of the screen is much more engaging than simply hearing a voice (see figure 20.3).

• **Be mindful of time parameters.** When you are beginning to create online lessons, it is helpful to have some sort of timer in front of you. This helps you to be more aware of the time parameters. Again, the online lesson is

Figure 20.2

much different in terms of pacing and length, from an in-person lesson. Again, online lessons should be two to eight minutes in duration.

• **Attend to pacing.** The lesson needs to be highly visual and briskly paced. The ideal time to spend on each slide is ten to thirty seconds. Keep in mind that students can pause the video at any time to take notes or listen again. The actual speed is dependent on your audience. Lessons for younger students need to be a bit slower.

• **Attend to pitch and modulation.** Show some enthusiasm for your topic. Modulate your voice. Include dramatic pauses. Do anything to keep the listeners' attention. Remember, you are competing with a whole host of Internet sensations: funny cat videos, celebrity gossip, and the latest sports information.

Reflecting

• **Watch your videos.** This may be hard to do at first; however, you must watch our teaching videos. Reviewing these lessons is the best way to get a sense of content and pacing. It is also a good way to find mistakes.

FINAL WORD

Technology is advancing at an expediential rate. There will be changes in the future of which we cannot now image. It is very likely that online teaching in some form will be a regular part of all teachers teaching repertoire at some

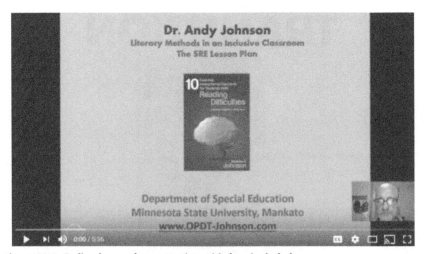

Figure 20.3 Online lesson demonstration with face included

point. However, today, online lessons can be used to help students review important skills or concepts, to keep students who are absent from missing important content, or to use to enhance current teaching practice as part of flipped instruction, learning centers, discovery learning, learning contracts, or other types of teaching and learning strategies.

Part VI

LITERACY

This section contains three chapters describing ways in which literacy can be used to enhance or extend learning:

Chapter 21

Learning Logs

A learning log is simply a blank notebook used to record students' thoughts, observations, and interesting ideas related to topics being studied. Learning logs can be used to manipulate, extend, apply, or reinforce content from a lesson or assigned reading.

CONTENT

What do students record in a learning log? Many of the strategies described in this book can be used to design learning log entries such as graphic organizers, thinking skills, Bloom's Taxonomy, and multiple intelligence theories. Other ideas included the following:

• **3-I.** After a lesson or reading an assigned text, ask students to identify what they consider to be the interesting or important ideas (3-I). This empowers students to make the decision as to what they think might be interesting or important. Also, this open-ended format enables students of all ability levels to succeed and at the same time, it provides insight as to how students are processing the new information. Encourage students to add pictures or diagrams to their 3-I chart.

• **Artistic prompt.** Instead of a written description, ask students to use a diagram or picture to describe something related to that day's class or assigned reading. This allows students to use artistic and visual-spatial intelligence in coming to know and describe an idea from class.

• **Vocabulary maps.** Students can create a vocabulary map for one to three words from the lesson or assigned reading. Vocabulary maps are graphic organizers used to add depth and breadth to students' understanding of words

(Johnson, 2016a). Various vocabulary maps usually ask for the target word, a definition, descriptors, and examples (see figure 21.1). Some forms also include a picture or diagram and an association.

• **The window.** Students create a window in their learning log related to the concept or skill being taught (see Table 21.3). On one side, they list two

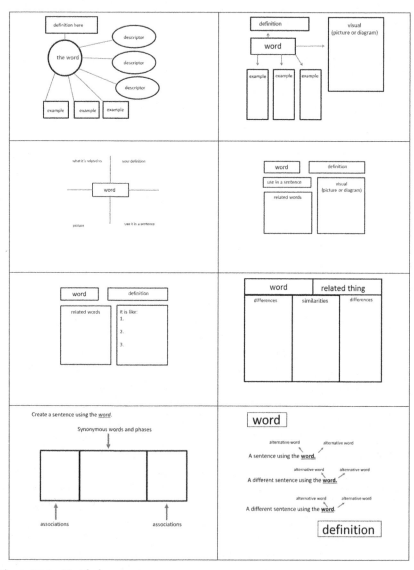

Figure 21.1   Vocabulary maps

Table 21.1 Window

Clear	Unclear
1.	1.
2.	2.

things that seem very clear and understandable. On the other side, they list two things that seem a bit unclear or hazy. Students then share their windows in small group. The very act of sharing ideas helps clarify some elements from the unclear side. To extend, the small groups then create a large window with three things on each side. This provides a form of formative assessment, enabling you to see what students know as well as what needs to be retaught or reviewed.

• **Discussions.** Learning logs are an effective tool to use with discussions. Given a discussion questions, students can write down some of their thoughts before large group or small group discussions. As well, after a T-talk or large group discussion, students can be directed to share their ideas in their learning log.

• **Ultra-personal connections.** Learning logs can be used to link the content being learned to students' personal experiences and to create vehicles for the exploration of social and emotional issues. Designing these kinds of activities and assignments takes a bit of creativity and the connections are not always direct; however, ultra-personal connection activities add depth and dimensions to students' learning and enable you to address the full continuum of the human experience. Ultra-personal connections enable students tell their stories or describe their ideas or experiences. They enable students to emote, imagine, remember, associate, or intuit related to a concept or topic being taught.

For example, Ms. Anderson's high school life science class was studying human interaction with disease-causing organisms. After a lesson, she asked her student to record one interesting or important idea from the lesson. Ms. Anderson then asked students to describe a person or situation in their life that causes them to feel dis-ease, lack of ease, or something that makes them feel nervous. Students spent the last five minutes of class sharing their ideas in small group.

TIPS

Three tips for using learning logs: First, learning logs should not be kept in students' desks or lockers. In this way, they do not become just another notebook that could be lost, torn, or used for homework. Instead, they should be kept in a special place on a shelf or in some container. Students can then be directed to get their learning logs at designated times. In a middle or high school settings, set them out for students to take as they enter the classroom at the beginning of class. Also, keeping the learning logs in a special place enables you to review, add remarks, or respond to students' entries outside of class.

Second, do not assign grades for spelling, mechanics, or even content in a learning log. The learning log is a learning tool not an evaluation tool. However, if you insist on assigning a grade, you can grade based on students' thinking or their regular participation.

And finally, show students the learning log prompt, activity, assignment, or question at the beginning of class. This enables them to select and process relevant information during class to use in responding at the end of the class.

SHARING ENTRIES

There are times when it is appropriate to share learning log entries. Here are four ways for this to be done:

• **Partner oral response.** Here students find a neighbor and read a learning log entry orally or simply describe some of the main ideas. Partners then respond orally to the ideas, again, using an aesthetic response.
• **Small group oral response.** In small groups, students read or describe a learning log entry. These entries become natural vehicles for small group discussions as members of the group respond orally with aesthetic response questions and comments.
• **Trade and respond.** Students trade learning logs with a partner and write their responses right on the learning log page. In this way, the learning log becomes a living entity and a collection of perspectives. In groups of three or more, students can keep rotating learning logs until everybody has responded to each.
• **Whole class.** Two or three volunteers sign up to share an idea or learning log entry with the whole class each day. Do no more than three of these whole class kinds of sharing in a given class period as students naturally get distracted after a few minutes of listening passively.

FINAL WORD

Learning logs can be used as an alternative to expensive, consumable workbooks and worksheets. They can be used to differentiation learning

Chapter 22

Strategies for Helping Students Read Textbooks and Other Types of Expository Text

In every classroom, there are students of varying reading levels. This chapter provides strategies that all teachers can use to enhance all students' ability levels to read textbooks and other expository (informational) text.

PRE-READING STRATEGIES

Pre-reading strategies are used to provide the support necessary for students to read the text independently (Johnson, 2016a). Very rarely should students be asked to read a text cold (without any sort of preparation). Below are described 11 pre-reading strategies. Each of these should take between one and no more than eight minutes.

1. **Activate relevant schemata**. Before reading, help students recall what they know about a subject. For example, before reading a chapter on amphibians, you would ask students, "What do we know about amphibians?" As students respond, their ideas are listed on a board, screen, or chart.

2. **Provide background information.** Using the headings of the text as an outline, teach the salient elements of what students are about to read.

3. **Use advanced organizers**. An advanced organizer is a graphic organizer shown in advance of the assigned reading or lesson. It shows the structure of what is to be read or learned (see figure 22.1). This could include an outline, graphic organizers such as concept maps and semantic maps, or even charts or diagrams. The level of detail contained in the advanced organizer should be commensurate with students' reading level and age. The structure and sequence of the information presented should replicate exactly that which is found in the text. These can be printed out in paper form, displayed on a board, or poster, or projected onto a screen.

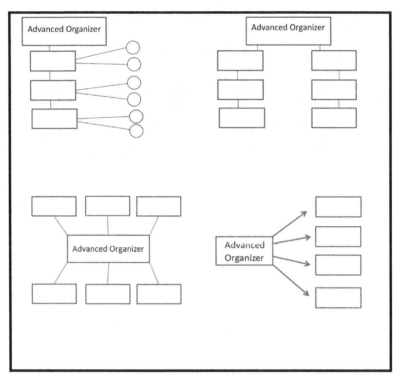

Figure 22.1 **Examples of advanced organizers**

4. **Guided notes.** Guided notes are outlines, semantic maps, or concept maps with spaces provided for students to insert notes as they are reading. Most often outlines are used here. Textbox 22.1 provides an example of what guided notes would look like for the section discussed further. To provide further scaffolding, the teacher could fill in parts of the outline for struggling readers.

TEACH STUDY SKILL STRATEGIES

1. The Strategies

a.   Five-step basic note-taking strategy.

   1.
   2.

b. Read, dot, and record.

　1.
　2.

c. Preview-overview.

　1.
　2.

d. Read and pause.

　1.
　2.

e. Paragraph reread.

　1.
　2.

f. Skim, reread, and note.

　1.
　2.

2. Tips

　a.
　b.

Textbox 22.1 Guided notes

5. **Present important vocabulary words**. Identify two to no more than six new or relatively unfamiliar words that are important in understanding the text. Present these words in the context of the sentence in which they are found in the text. Display the sentences so that all can see. Read them through with students, and help them generate at least two possible synonymous words or phrases (if possible). Then provide short mini-lessons to teach the necessary conceptual knowledge.

6. **Short related discussion.** Design a short small group or whole class discussion related to something found in the text (see chapter 14). Questions should be linked to the upcoming text in such a way that the discussion illuminates the text and the text illuminates the discussion topic.

7. **List, group, and organize**. This is an activity for large group, small groups, or pairs. Before reading, ask students to identify and list what they know about the text topic. Their ideas should be listed on a screen, poster, or board for large group. Paper or computer can be used for small groups and pairs. To ensure there is an adequate breadth of knowledge, the teacher can also include information on this list related to text. Next, ask students to use inductive analysis to put the ideas into groups. Finally, have students use the information to create a graphic organizer (see figure 23.1). As a postreading activity, students can (a) add additional information to their graphic organizer, (b) revise or make corrections to their graphic organizer, or (c) create a new graphic organizer. For younger students, you will need to provide the groups and headings for them after the list has been created. They would then put the ideas in the correct group.

8. **What's my topic?** This strategy is designed to activate relevant schemata in a game-like format. The topic of the upcoming text should be a mystery (this activity may not work with a textbook chapter). Students are put in small groups. After a clue is given, each group, in turn, asks a yes/no

Keywords	Clues
1.	
2.	
3.	
4.	
5.	
6.	
7.	
8.	
Text topic prediction:	

Figure 22.2   Graphic organizer for semantic impression

Table 22.1   Confirmations

	Agree	Disagree
1. Lizards are amphibians.		
2. Frogs cool themselves by opening their mouth.		
3. Salamanders only live in North America.		
4. Some frogs and can live to be twenty years old.		
5. A lizard is the same as a salamander.		

question and attempts to guess the mystery topic. Keep going until one group correctly guesses the topic and wins the game.

9. **Semantic impression.** This also works best for reading expository text that is not part of an assigned textbook. Here a list of eight to ten key-words and phrases are presented to students. Students are asked to make a prediction of an upcoming reading topic. Remember, a prediction is not simply a guess; rather, a guess based on clues. Use the graphic organizer in figure 22.2 to list the keywords and clues. This can be done in large and small groups and pairs. The discussion that occurs in these small groups provides opportunities for students to interact with words and concepts they will encounter in the text.

10. **Confirmations.** Before reading, present students with three to five declarative statements that can be confirmed by reading the upcoming selection. Students should be asked to agree or disagree with each of the statements before reading (see table 22.1). They should revise confirmations as needed after reading. Again, the conversation that occurs as a result makes this an excellent activity for pairs and small groups.

TEACH STUDY SKILL STRATEGIES

A study skill strategy is a process used to create meaning with expository text (textbooks). For students to use them, they have to be easy to use and practical. The following are seven such strategies. These should be taught explicitly and reviewed every year.

The Strategies

• **Five-step basic note-taking strategy.** Guided notes (discussed above) is a good introduction to note taking. This provides the structure necessary for students to develop their own note-taking strategy. Then teach a very basic form of note taking. Keep it simple. Students will naturally develop more complex forms of note taking as the need arises.

The five-step basic note-taking strategy

a. Write the title of the article or chapter on top of the page.
b. Write the name of the heading (underline it).
c. As you read each paragraph, select only the most important ideas.
d. Record the idea using short, abbreviated (incomplete) sentences.
e. Recording supporting ideas for following sentences:

- Use numerals for main ideas
- Use small letters for supporting ideas
- Less confusing than official "outlining" formats

- **Read, dot, and record.** When reading expository text, you sometimes do not want to interrupt the reading flow by stopping to record notes. Instead, put a dot in the margin of the text with a pencil to identify important

First Paragraph	Last Paragraph

Headings and Notes

Figure 22.3   Graphic organizer for preview-overview

ideas as you are reading. (You can erase the dots later.) After reading, go back and take notes using the five-step basic note-taking strategy discussed above.

• **Preview-overview.** Start by reading the first paragraph, the headings and subheading, and the last paragraph. Then read the entire text and take notes. The graphic organizer in figure 22.3 can be used to teach this process. The first two sections are used to list ideas found in the first and last paragraphs. The last section is used for notes.

• **Read and pause.** First read a paragraph. Then pause to see if you understood and can restate an important idea. If so, resume reading. If not, return and reread.

• **Paragraph reread.** Read a paragraph. Then skim to find an important idea. Continue.

• **3 x 5 card.** A 3 x 5 card helps to keep you focused as you read. Some prefer to put the card on top of the line they are reading and move down. This allows their eyes to naturally predict and move ahead. Others prefer to put the card underneath the line they're reading. This can also be used in conjunction with any of the strategies described earlier.

• **Skim, reread, and note.** Quickly skim the text to get a sense of the whole. Then they Reread and take notes as you read.

Take Notes	*Dot and Notes*	*Preview/Overview*	*Skim, Re-read, and Note*
1. Record heading	1. Read a paragraph.	1. Look at the title and headings.	1. Quickly skim read the article/chapter.
2. Read a paragraph.	2. Put dot next to important ideas	2. Read the first paragraph and last paragraphs.	2. Re-read the article/chapter.
3. Record important ideas	3. Finish chapter	3. Read the article/chapter.	3. Note or record important ideas.
4. Use numbers and letters	4. Take notes using outline and headings	4. Take notes.	
Paragraph Re-Read	*3'x5' Card*	*Read and Pause*	
1. Read each paragraph quickly.	1. Put a card on top/bottom of sentence	1. Read a paragraph.	
2. Re-read to find important sentences or ideas.	2. Move slowly ahead as you read	2. Pause and check. (Do I understand?)	
3. Continue.		3. Return or resume.	

Figure 22.4   Poster ideas for study skill strategies

Tips for Teaching Study Skill Strategies

Starting at the beginning of each year, teach one or two of the study skill strategies described in this section. Keep it simple and practical, adopt and adapt, and encourage students to use the strategies that work best for them. Also, create a poster to display the study skill strategies that you will teach in your classes (see figure 22.4). Break each study skill strategy into specific steps. When assigning a text, always remind students to use one of these study skill strategies.

FINAL WORD

All teachers should be teachers of reading in some form. This chapter described eleven prereading strategies that can be used to prepare students to read expository text. It also described seven simple study skill strategies that can be used to help students create meaning with expository text.

Chapter 23

All Teachers Are Teachers of Writing

All teachers, at all levels, who ask students to do any sort of writing should know how to teach writing. However, in an attempt to teach writing, two things often occur that are not very effective. First, teachers simply describe what the finished product should look like (Johnson, 2016b). That is, instruction is related only to grammar, punctuation, and other mechanics. And second, teachers or instructors just assign more writing. If you want to help students become better writers, you must teach them the process (Johnson, 2008). This chapter presents the five-step writing process and some tips for teaching each step.

THE FIVE-STEP WRITING PROCESS

Each step of the five-step writing process described further must be explicitly taught and modeled.

- **Step 1—Prewriting**. The goal here is to generate ideas. Listing, brainstorming, outlining, silent thinking, conversation with a neighbor, or power writing (described below) are all ways to generate ideas.
- **Step 2—Drafting**. Drafting is the writer's first attempt to capture ideas on paper. Quantity here is valued over quality. If done correctly, the draft is a rambling, disconnected accumulation of ideas. The draft is like throwing a large blob of clay on a potter's spinning wheel. The goal is to simply get clay on the wheel or ideas on the page.
- **Step 3—Revising**. Here a piece is revised and reshaped many times. This is like a potter beginning to mold and shape the blob of clay on the wheel to make a pot. The pot does not appear with one spin of the wheel. It

begins to appear over time with much shaping. Revising writing is similar. Here you shape the text, add parts, take parts away, and continue to mold and change it. You reread paragraphs, move things around, and look for flow and structure. Revising occurs over time and is at the heart of the writing process.

• **Step 4—Editing**. This is the step where grammar, spelling, and punctuation errors are corrected. A word of caution: the quickest way to ruin a good writing project or damage a writer is to insist that Step 4 be Step 1, 2, or 3. If writers are editing or worrying about mechanics at the prewriting, drafting, and revising stages, the flow of ideas and the quality of writing suffers. Precious brain space that is devoted to generating and connecting ideas will instead be used instead to worry about writing mechanics.

One last thing about the editing phase: teach your students how to use the grammar and spelling functions on a word processor and set up peer editing groups.

• **Step 5—Publishing and sharing**. This is where students' writing is shared with an audience. Writing becomes real and alive at this point. At this step, you are limited only by your imagination. Publishing can involve putting together class books, collections of writing, websites, online publishing, school or class newspapers, magazines, or displaying short samples of writing in the hall or out in the community. As well, writing experiences can be shared by having students read their work out loud to another classmate, in small groups, or in a large group setting.

STRATEGIES FOR PREWRITING, DRAFTING, REVISING, EDITING, AND PUBLISHING

This section describes strategies and activities for each phase of the five-step writing process.

Prewriting Strategies for Generating Ideas for Writing

Prewriting strategies should be used to generate idea before students begin writing their drafts. Put the steps for these strategies on a bulletin board or poster form to use as a teaching guide and reminder (see figure 23.1).

• **Power write.** With these prewriting strategies, students write continuously for one to three minutes. This is different from the free write where students generally write at a slower pace for five to ten minutes. The power write is designed to get students to write quickly without thinking. Evaluating

Power Write

1. Find an idea.
2. List first word or image that comes to mind.
3. Write quickly; keep the pencil moving.
4. Write for 2-3 minutes.
5. Look for ideas to use.
6. Begin drafting.

Brainstorm and Group

1. Start with a topic.
2. Generate as ideas as you can.
3. Look for groups or patterns.
4. Organize into groups.
5. Use groups for sections or paragraphs.
6. Begin drafting

Outlining

1. Look at topic or theme.
2. List important ideas using numbers.
3. Use letters to add details.
4. Begin drafting

Web and Brainstorm

1. Find a writing topic (central bubble).
2. Identify 2-4 sub-ideas (nodes).
3. Brainstorm on each node.
4. Each node becomes a paragraph
5. Begin drafting.

Brainstorm

1. Look at the idea.
2. List as many ideas as quickly as you can.
3. Begin drafting

Turn to a Neighbor

1. Find a topic or theme.
2. Turn to a neighbor and share.
3. Listen, ask questions, add ideas.
4. Begin drafting

List-Four

1. Start with an idea.
2. Quickly list 3-5 words that come to your mind on top of your page.
3. Begin writing.

Figure 23.1 Prewriting strategies

ideas gets in the way of idea generation and should be avoided. Here you want students to make quick associations. To do this, students start with a writing topic (or any word idea) and quickly write down the first idea that comes to mind. They should keep their pencil moving, recording ideas, and freely hopping from one idea to the next. If done correctly, the writing should be a jumbled and disjointed mess. You will need to demonstrate how to do this by thinking aloud as you record your ideas.

• **Brainstorm and group.** Start with a writing topic, students list as many related things as they can. This is different from the power write in that students simply list a word to hold individual ideas. Whereas, in power writing, students record complete ideas and sentence parts. Once all ideas are listed, then students should start looking for groups or patterns to emerge. Similar

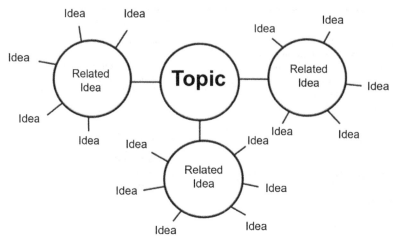

Figure 23.2   Web and brainstorm

ideas should be put together to create groups. Again, the teacher will need to demonstrate how to brainstorm and group by doing one together and thinking aloud as you do it.

• **Outlining.** With older writers, outlining begins after research has produced a set of notes. Students start with the writing topic, then look for two to four main ideas related to the topic. Identifying supporting details for each of the main ideas becomes much easier once a flexible outline has been created. As students are working through the draft and revision stages, new ideas should be allowed to appear and old ideas to melt away, merge, or appear in other places.

• **Web and brainstorm.** Web and brainstorm provides the same type of structure as an outline, however, it is more spatial and more visually stimulating for some (see figure 23.2). Here you start with a writing topic as a central bubble, then look for two to four related ideas for the nodes.

• **Brainstorm.** The goal in brainstorming is generating a large quantity of ideas without evaluating any of them. Students, do not naturally know how to brainstorm, thus you must teach and demonstrate the process. If everyone is writing on a similar topic, brainstorming can be an effective prewriting activity to do in a large group. As students see the ideas of others, they get more ideas for their own writing project. There are four rules for brainstorming. Put these rules in poster form to assist in your initial brainstorming instruction, and then use this poster for quick review when needed.

RULES FOR BRAINSTORMING

- All ideas must be accepted. No criticizing or evaluation is allowed. At this stage, bad ideas are just as important as good ideas.
- Freewheeling is celebrated. Creative, bizarre, unusual, and silly ideas are welcomed along with smart aleck comments and random associations. These can all be used to stretch our thinking and get us thinking more broadly.
- The goal of brainstorming is quantity. The more ideas we have, the greater our choice is in finding a solution.
- Hitchhiking is welcome. Hitchhiking is when you add to an idea that has already been stated or combine two or more ideas. This is a technique many creative problem solvers use.

Textbox 23.1

- **Turn to a neighbor.** Explaining our initial ideas or listening to the ideas of others is a simple, effective prewriting strategy. For example, I might say, *"Today we're writing about things we noticed on the way to school. Take a minute, turn to a neighbor. Share at least two things you noticed on the way to school."* Or, *"Think about what you might want to write about today. Turn to a neighbor and share at least three ideas related to your writing topic."*
- **List-four.** The last prewriting strategy is list four. Here you start with an idea or writing topic, then quickly list four words or ideas associated with the writing topic on top of the page before writing.

The Draft—Sloppy Copy

The draft (sometimes called a sloppy copy) is students' initial thinking space where they make the first attempt to capture their ideas on paper. You cannot assume that students know how to do this. You must teach and model how to create a draft. Do this by creating a draft in front of your students, thinking aloud as you do so. Also, show them handwritten drafts that are sloppy with lots of scratches, crossed out words and ideas, arrows, and other diagrams in the margins.

Having students respond to each other's drafts makes them become alive and meaningful and provides the writer ideas for the revision stage. You cannot assume at any level that students know how to respond to drafts. The following are three simple ideas for responding to drafts:

- **Partner oral response.** Here students turn to a neighbor and read their story draft out loud. They could also simply describe some of the main ideas. The partner then responds orally to the ideas. You will, however, have to teach students how to respond to each other's writing in a positive, supportive manner. The response guidelines can be used here. Select three to five and put them on a poster to use as a reference. Tell students that these are just hints if they don't know what to say.

Response guidelines

1. I liked _____.
2. I want to know more about _____.
3. _____ might make it more interesting.
4. I reminds me of _____.
5. _____ was very clear.
6. I am confused about _____.
7. I don't understand _____.
8. You could think about adding _____.
9. It reminded me of _____.
10. I think that _____ is interesting.

Textbox 23.2

• **Small group oral response**. In small groups, students read or describe all or part of a draft. Group members should be given guidelines to find two things they like and two things that could be added or done differently (with younger students, it would be one thing).

• **Trade and respond**. Students trade writing drafts with a partner and write their response right on the page. You can also use groups of three or more students, having them write and rotate papers until everybody has responded to each. In this way, the draft becomes a living entity with a collection of perspectives.

Revising

Once a student has taken a piece to the revision stage, the majority of time should be spent reading, rereading, moving things around, getting feedback from others. This is where the writer molds and shapes a piece of writing. Encourage students to read their work out loud to develop a writer's ear.

• **Magic circle.** The magic circle is a strategy that enables students get feedback from peers during the revising process. The goal of this feedback is to see how the writing is playing in the head of the readers. It can be used with students as young as second grade all the way up to graduate school. The steps are as follows:

1. Before beginning, tell students that the magic circle is not for editing or correcting mistakes. They are to respond to ideas found on papers.
2. Students identify a piece of writing for which they would like a response. Papers should not have names on so that students' writing is anonymous.
3. Collect students' writing.
4. With elementary students (2nd through 5th grade), move the desks in a circle facing inward. The teacher stands inside the circle and directs action. (With middle students and older, desks can remain in place.)
5. After shuffling the papers, give one to each student. Students respond to that paper, letting the writer know what thoughts were going through their head as they read it. Direct students to "think all over the paper" with their pencils. They should write on the paper, making marks and arrows to show exactly what they liked or wanted to know more about.
6. When students finish responding to a paper, they leave the paper on the desk, move to the center of the circle and wait for an empty desk. They then move to that desk and respond to that paper. With middle school and high school students, desks do not have to be moved into circles. Instead, when students finish responding to a paper, they simply hold it in the air and trade with another student. The goal for younger students should be to respond to at least three papers (this takes a lot of concentration). The goal for older students is to get respond to four papers. Sessions varying in duration from ten minutes for younger student to usually no more than thirty minutes for older students.
7. Watch your students. When you see the energy starting to lag, instruct them to finish the paper they are on and return it to a front table or a spot that you have designated in front of the room.
8. When all papers are returned, students can then come up and find their own. They will find a paper that is alive with the thoughts and ideas of others.
   Again, it is important to remind students that this is a revising strategy, not an editing strategy. Revising is finished when students feel the writing is as they want it to be. Only then should they focus on editing.

Editing

At the editing stage, students fix grammar, spelling, and punctuation errors. Two important points to reinforce here: First, good writing is not writing without errors. Good writing is having good ideas and then communicating them

Table 23.1 Editing checklist for elementary students

	Yes	No
1. Begins sentences with capital letters.		
2. Sentences are a complete idea.		
3. Ends sentences with period.		
4. Circles words that don't look quite right (spelling).		
5. Uses "isn't" and "wasn't" correctly.		

effectively. Grammar, spelling, and punctuation are used to help writers communicate their ideas. Second, let your students know that all writers need and use editors.

- **Self-editing.** Teach students how to edit their own work by providing structure in the form of a simple checklist (see table 23.1). Editing checklists for elementary students should include three to five elements. Checklists for middle school students and above can include more; however, do not make this a laundry list. Keep it focused. Use it to reinforce the skills being taught as part of your writing curriculum. As well, you can create different checklists for different students in your class, depending on what you wish them to focus on.
- **Peer-editing—SET.** Peer-editing is a way for students to edit each other's papers. Editing other students' papers is also an indirect way to learn about spelling, grammar, and punctuation. SET stands for **skill expert tables** (SET). The steps are as follows:
  1. Designate a day or date for the editing of papers. Encourage students to have something ready to edit on that day. For example, Fridays could be editing days.
  2. Identify three to eight skills related to grammar, spelling, or punctuation upon which to focus. Assign a table for each skill focus area.
  3. Assign students to editing tables where they can become experts in the use of a specific skill. Assign each student in the class to a table. For example, a spelling table would look just for spelling errors. Another table could be the sentence table looking for complete sentences with capital letters and periods. Another table could be the "there-their and too-to-two table checking to see that these are used correctly. Depending on your teaching or tutoring situation, assign two to four students to each editing table. Sometimes a parent volunteer, paraprofessional, or older student can be used to assist the work at each table. In these cases, they should intervene

as little as possible. Real learning occurs when students discuss, communicating, and explain their thinking relative to a particular skill.

4. Papers in need of editing are passed out to the different tables. Editing tables examine and edit each paper looking only at their specific editing element.

5. When a paper is finished at one table, it is passed on to the next editing table until it completes all tables.

• **Peer-editing—PET.** PET stands for professional editing tables (PET). The steps are as follows:

1. Designate one table for editing.

2. During the writing time, students who have completed revising their papers do an initial edit on their own.

3. When they have completed their own editing, students bring their piece to the professional editing. Here a parent, paraprofessional, or older student works along with two or three voluntary editors. Every student should have a chance to be an editor. This is one of the best ways to learn about grammar, spelling, and punctuation.

4. Use a checklist to remind student-editors of the things to look for. table 23.2 provides an example of what this might look like. Examine

Table 23.2 Checklist for PET

Things to Check
1. SENTENCES
a. The writer uses complete sentences.
b. The sentences are easy to read.
c. The sentences of capital letters and periods at the end.
2. PARAGRAPHS
a. Ideas are organized into paragraphs.
b. Paragraphs are used to start a new idea.
c. Paragraphs are indented at the beginning.
3. SPELLING
a. The writer uses spell-check on questionable words.
b. The writer spells contractions, such as isn't, wasn't, can't, didn't, and they're, correctly.
c. The writer uses there, their, and they're correctly.

students' papers to decide the specific elements to use in creating your own.

Also, in deciding what skills to teach, it is most effective to look at their papers, to see what types of errors seem to be reoccurring. Create short lessons to teach those skills. Then create a checklist including these skills in the editing process.

Publishing/Sharing

Teachers should not be the only audience for students' work. Publishing/ sharing refers to any situation where students get eyeballs or ears on their writing. There are a variety of ways create audiences for students' writing. Three common methods are presented here:

Author's chair. Authors chair is where one or two students read all or a portion of their work to the whole class.

• **Student books or collections**. Depending on the age of your students, you can create collections of students work to be read by other students. These could be expository text on specific subjects that you are studying, or they could include stories that could be read for reading practice.

• **Websites and online newspapers.** Students writing here can be organized by date, age, and topic. This enables students writing to be shared with parents or put in an electronic portfolio to demonstrate writing competency.

FINAL WORD

Learning to write and writing well is not difficult if you know and understand the process. This chapter described the five-step writing process and provided strategies for each step.

Conclusion

The Science, Art, and Craft of Teaching

Teaching is a science, an art, and a craft.

- **A science.** It is a science in that there are strategies and practices that a body of research has shown to be effective in enhancing learning. Just like doctors, teachers should use research to inform their practice. On the individual level, teaching is a science also in that teachers are constantly collecting data by observing their students in order to see if learning is taking place and how they learn best. And, like scientists, teachers experiment with new techniques or strategies to see how they work.

- **An art.** It is an art in that teachers must bring themselves fully into their teaching. As a teacher, you will need to find the methods and strategies that work best for you. Teachers are not standardized products. What works for one teacher may not work for another. Thus, all the teaching strategies that you learn should be adopted and adapted to fit your particular teaching situation and your personal teaching style. To be an effective teacher, you must carve out your own teaching philosophy and discover your own unique talents and learn how to use them.

- **A craft**. Teaching might also be described as a craft. A craft is a skill or set of skills learned through experience. This is exactly what teaching is. This means that one cannot expect to leave a college teacher preparation program as a finished teaching product. Teaching is a complex, multidimensional endeavor; not something that can be mastered in four semesters. Master teachers develop over time through experience and continued study and reflection. Undergraduate and postbaccalaureate teacher preparation programs will not teach you how to teach; instead, they will give you the basis upon which to learn how to teach. Does this mean teacher education programs are of little value? Certainly not. There is a fairly substantial body of research that indicates that teacher education programs improve teachers' performance and their students' achievement (Wilson, Floden, & Ferrini-Mundy, 2001). However, becoming a master teacher happens over time with continued professional development and reflection. Hopefully, this book can become one small part of this development and reflection.

Andrew P. Johnson, Ph.D.
Minnesota State University, Mankato
Mankato, MN 56001

References

Ausubel, D. P. (1977). The facilitation of meaningful verbal learning in the classroom. *Educational Psychologist, 12*, 162–178.

Borich, G. D. (2004). *Effective teaching methods* (5th ed.). Upper Saddle River, NJ: Pearson.

Bruer, J. T. (1999). *Schools for thought: A science of learning in the classroom.* Cambridge, MA: MIT Press.

Bruner, J. (1977). *The process of education.* Boston, MA: Harvard University Press.

Cazden, C. B. (1998). *Classroom discourse: The language of teaching and learning.* Portsmouth, NH: Heinemann Educational Books.

Darling-Hammond, L. (1999). *Teacher quality and study achievement: A review of state policy evidence.* Seattle, WA: Center for the Study of Teaching and Policy, University of Washington.

Darling-Hammond, L., Holtzman, D. J., Gatlin, S. J., & Heilig, J. V. (2005). Does teacher certification matter? *Evidence about teacher certification, Teach for America, and teacher effectiveness.* Chapel Hill, NC: The Southeast Center for Teaching Quality.

Darling-Hammond, L., Youngs, P. (2002). Defining "highly qualified teachers": What does "scientifically-based research" actually tell us? *Educational Researcher, 31*(9), 13–25.

Diaz-Lefebvre, R. (2006). Learning for understanding: A faculty-driven paradigm shift in learning, imaginative teaching, and creative assessment. *Community College Journal of Research & Practice, 30*, 135–137.

Eggen, P., & Kauchak, D. (2001). *Strategies for teachers: Teaching content and thinking skills* (4th ed.). Needham Heights, MA: Allyn and Bacon.

Eggen, P. & Kauchak, D. (2007). *Educational psychology: Windows on classrooms.* Upper Saddle River, NJ: Pearson.

Gardner, H. (1993). *Multiple Intelligences: The theory in practice.* New York: Basic Books.

Good, T., & Brophy, J. (1995). *Contemporary educational psychology* (5th ed.). White Plains, NY: Longman.

Gorski, P. (2000). The challenge of defining a single "multicultural education." Retrieved from www.mhhe.com/socscience/education/multi/define.html

Jarolimek, J., Foster, Sr., C. D., & Kellough, R. D. (2005). *Teaching and learning in the elementary school* (8th ed.). Upper Saddle River, NJ: Pearson.

Jensen, E. (2000). Moving with the brain in mind. *Educational Leadership, 58,* 34–37.

Johnson, A. (2000). *Up and out: Using creative and critical thinking skills to enhance learning.* Boston, MA: Allyn and Bacon.

Johnson, A. (2008). *Teaching reading and writing: Research-based strategies for teachers, tutors, parents, and paraprofessionals.* Lanham, MD: Rowman and Littlefield.

Johnson, A. (2009). *Making connections in elementary and middle school social studies* (2nd ed.). Thousand Oaks, CA: SAGE.

Johnson, A. (2016a). *10 essential instruction elements for students with reading difficulties: A brain friendly approach.* Thousand Oaks, CA: Corwin.

Johnson, A. (2016b). *Academic writing: Process and product.* Lanham, MD: Rowman and Littlefield.

Kornhaber, M. (2004). Multiple intelligences: From the ivory tower to the dusty classroom: But why? *Teachers College Record, 106,* 67–76.

Lukinsky, J., & Schachter, L. (1998). Questions in human and classroom discourse. Coalition for the Advancement of Jewish Education. Retrieved from http://www.caje.org

Marzano, R. J., Pickering, D. J., & Pollock, J. E. (2001). *Classroom instruction that works: Research-based strategies for increasing student achievement.* Alexandria, VI: ASCD.

Maslow, A. (1971). *The farther reaches of human nature.* New York: Viking Press.

Mayer, R. E. & Wittrock M. C. (2006). Problem solving. In P. Alexander & P. Winne (Eds.). *Handbook of educational psychology* (6th ed.) (pp. 287–304). Mahwah, NJ: Lawrence Erlbaum Associates.

National Research Council. (2000). *How people learn: brain, mind, experience, and school.* Washington, DC: National Academies Press.

Ormrod, J. E. (2006). *Essentials of educational psychology.* Upper Saddle River, NJ: Pearson.

Ormrod, J. E. (2012). *Human learning* (6th ed.). Boston, MA: Pearson.

Perry, N. E., Turner, J. C., & Meyer, D. K. (2006). Classrooms as context for motivating learning. In P. Alexander and P. Winne (Eds.). *Handbook of educational psychology* (6th ed.) (pp. 327–348). Mahwah, NJ: Lawrence Erlbaum Associates.

Porter, A. C., Youngs, P., & Odden, A. (2001). Advances in teacher assessment and their uses. In V. Richardson (Ed.), *Handbook of research on teaching* (pp. 259–297). Washington, DC: American Educational Research Association.

Pressley, M., Harris, K. R., & Marks, M. B. (1992). But good strategy users are constructivists! *Educational Psychology Review, 4,* 3–31.

Rogers, C. R. & Freiberg, H. J. (1994). *Freedom to learn* (3rd ed.). Columbus, OH: Merrill/Macmillan.

Sadker, D., Sadker, M., & Zittleman, K. R. (2008). *Teachers, schools, and society* (8th ed.). New York, NY: McGrall-Hill.

Santrock, J. (2010). *Educational psychology* (5th ed.) New York, NY: McGraw-Hill.

Sternberg, R. J. & Grigorenka, E. (2000). *Teaching for successful intelligence.* Arlington Heights, IL: Skylight Professional Development.

Sternberg, R. J. & Williams, W. M. (2002). *Educational psychology.* Boston, MA: Allyn and Bacon.

Sternberg, R. J. & Williams, W. M. (2010). *Educational psychology* (2nd ed.). Upper Saddle, NJ: Merrill.

Tomlinson, C. (1995). *How to differentiate instruction in mixed-ability classrooms.* Alexandria, VA: ASCD.

Tomlinson, C. (1999). *The differentiated classroom: Responding to the needs of all learners.* Alexandria, VA: ASCD.

Tomlinson, C. A. (2001). *How to differentiate instruction in a mixed-ability classroom* (2nd ed.). Alexandria, VA: ASCD.

Wilson, S. M., Floden, R., & Ferrini-Mundy, J. (2001). *Teacher preparation research: Current knowledge, gaps, and recommendations.* A research report prepared for the U.S. Department of Education. Seattle: Center for the Study of Teaching and Policy, University of Washington.

Woolfolk, A. (2007). *Educational psychology* (10th ed.). Boston, MA: Pearson

Woolfolk, A. (2015). *Educational psychology* (13th ed). Boston, MA: Pearson.

Zeichner, K. & Liston, D. (1996). *Reflective teaching.* Hillsdale, NJ: Erlbaum.

Index

About the Author

Dr. Andrew Johnson is a professor of literacy at Minnesota State University, Mankato, where he specializes in literacy instruction for struggling readers and students with intellectual disabilities. He also works with schools to design practical interventions and RTI plans for struggling readers. He worked for nine years in the public schools as an elementary teacher, gifted education coordinator, and wrestling coach before moving into higher education. He is the author of many books and articles related to literacy, teaching pedagogy, and other educational topics.

For instructional material and videos as well as information related to professional development opportunities, go to: www.OPDT-Johnson.com

To contact Dr. Johnson, email him at: Andrew.johnson@mnsu.edu

Made in the USA
Monee, IL
25 August 2023

41616775R00114